CATHOLIC PARISHES IN TRANSITION

CREATING VIABLE PARISHES THROUGH MERGERS, CLOSURES AND COLLABORATIONS

BY

REV. MACIEJ MANKOWSKI, D.MIN.

SEPTEMBER 2016

Based on the Dissertation

Journeying Together in Christ As a Viable Parish Community, Pastoral Recommendations for Merging, Closing and Collaborating of Catholic Parishes Based on Selected Case Studies from the Diocese of Youngstown, Ohio

Contact:
Rev. Maciej Mankowski, D.Min.
St. Joseph Catholic Church
427 E. Broadway
Alliance, OH 44601
phone: (330) 821-5760
email: mmankowski@youngstowndiocese.org

The cover photo shows the reredos wooden mosaic in the sanctuary of St. Joseph Church in Alliance, Ohio. This picture was provided by Michael Skolosh Photography.

Dedication

I dedicate this book to all priests, pastors, parish administrators and lay parish leaders who had been tasked with the tremendous responsibility of overseeing and implementing parish structural changes. Their courage, honesty, hard work, dedication and sacrificial ministry of service have been an inspiration for this book. May the good Lord continue to bless you and watch over the people of God who have been entrusted to your pastoral care. As ministers of God's love, mercy, and compassion, may we always remember the words of Saint John Paul II: "Be Not Afraid!" Indeed, with God at our side and committed disciples and active parishioners, all things are possible. God does not only call to follow Him those who are ready. God calls the willing! May we always be willing to preach the Good News of the Gospel and to proclaim with our hearts, actions and lips that Christ has died, that He is risen and that one day He shall come back again.

In a special way, I dedicate this book to all Catholic women. They are the most loving and giving members of the Church whose passion and involvement in the life of Catholic parishes has been inspiring and life changing.

To Cathy and Angela for walking with me on this journey of life and faith. Your love and compassion, your ongoing support and words of wisdom helped me not only to accomplish this book but also inspired me to become a better priest and a more committed disciple of the Lord.

To Fr. Chris for your patience, insightful comments, pastoral wisdom and words of encouragement. I am very blessed to have friends like you in my life and I give thanks to God for allowing us to cross our paths and to minister to God's people in the Diocese of Youngstown.

Preface

Catholic parishes in the United States have been going through some major structural changes in the last couple of decades. The merging, closing and collaborating of parishes has become an undeniable part of the Catholic landscape in the United States. With the declining number of priests and religious as well as the significant shifts in the demographics of the Catholic population, the number of parishes without a resident pastor continues to grow. Furthermore, closed, merged and collaborating parishes have been on the rise, and they will continue in the years to come mainly in the Northeast and the Midwest parts of the country. The aim of this book is to develop helpful pastoral recommendations for pastors and parish leaders who oversee the process of closing, merging and collaborating of parishes. In addition, this book will present a concise historical development of Catholic parishes in connection with its canonical rights and obligations. The theological and theoretical aspects of this book will serve as a way to offer some insights into what it means to be a member of a parish community. No parish can survive without a specific mission and vision for the future. This book will offer some practical ideas used to assess various parish ministries and the overall vibrancy of a parish community. First hand experiences of pastors and parish leaders will be used in order to understand how parish mergers, closures and collaborations affect all parties involved in this process and to point out some recommended and discouraged pastoral practices.

CREATING THE CHURCH OF TOMORROW
A prayer by Archbishop Oscar Romero, (1917- 1980)

It helps, now and then, to step back and take a long view.

The Kingdom is not only beyond our efforts; it is even beyond our vision. We accomplish in our lifetime only a tiny fraction of the magnificent enterprise that is God's work.

Nothing we do is complete, which is a way of saying that the kingdom always lies beyond us.

No statement says all that could be said.

No prayer fully expresses our faith.

No confession brings perfection.

No pastoral visit brings wholeness.

No program accomplishes the church's mission.

No set of goals and objectives includes everything.

This is what we are about.

We plant the seeds that one day will grow.

We water seeds already planted, knowing that they hold future promises. We lay foundations that will need further development.

We provide yeast that produces far beyond our capabilities.

We cannot do everything, and there is a sense of liberation, in realizing that.

This enables us to do something, and to do it very well.

It may be incomplete, but it is a beginning, a step along the way, an opportunity for the Lord's grace to enter and do the rest.

We may never see the end results, but that is the difference between the master builder and the worker.

We are workers, not master builders; ministers not messiahs.

We are prophets of a future not our own.

Amen.

Table of Contents

CHAPTER I.

INTRODUCTION

Demographic Problem

Nowadays, it is not entirely uncommon to hear the sad news about yet another church closing, parish merging, clustering or forming a collaborative unit model. Many Roman Catholic dioceses in the United States have introduced various reconfiguration plans which focus on the restructuring and downsizing of the number of existing churches and parishes. The process of closing, merging and collaborating of parishes is hardly a recent development. In the last fourteen years, this painful sign of our times has become a sad reality for many parishes in the United States. According to the report presented by the Emerging Models of Pastoral Leadership: "In the last decade (2000-2010) the number of Catholic parishes in the United States has been reduced by 1,359 parishes – a decline of 7.1 percent."[1]

The issue at hand is that pastors, parish leaders and parishioners are significantly affected by this experience on different levels. Many of us have heard horror stories connected with a church closing or numerous parish mergers that almost started World War III. When emotions run high, feelings get hurt, and a bitter taste remains in the mouths of those who had lost the church of their ancestors and who had been encouraged or forced to join another parish. The issue at hand is connected with people and also with the process used to address the reality of this topic. A significant amount of time and effort need to be given to the pastoral planning and listening phases of this process. The clearer the strategic plan of implementation and the more frequent the communication between the diocese, pastor, parish leaders and parishioners, the better the final outcomes. It goes without saying that transparency and ongoing dialogue between all parties involved in the process of reconfiguration are essential elements that warrant success in the midst of many challenges connected with this endeavor.

Goals and Aims of this Book

The primary focus of this book is to present some pastoral recommendations and hopefully viable existing pastoral plans based on experiences connected with the successful and unsuccessful mergers, closures and collaborations of Catholic parishes. In order to raise awareness and sensitivity of pastors, parish leaders and parishioners faced with the possibility of parish merger, closure or collaboration, the author of this book will present the recommended pastoral practices regarding this process. Moreover, elements of the process requiring pastoral sensitivity will be emphasized. An in-depth analysis of this process is based on available theological and non-theological literature as well as personal experiences of parish leaders and

---

[1] Mark M. Gray, Mary L. Gautier and Melissa A. Cidade, "The Changing Face of U.S. Catholic Parishes," *Emerging Models of Pastoral Leadership Series* (Washington, DC: National Association for Lay Ministry, 2011), 6.

parishioners who were actively engaged in this undertaking. The author of this book wishes to share some practical recommendations for pastors and parish administrators, who may find themselves presently or in the future, as leaders of a parish community going through a transition while merging, closing and collaborating. This book is also aimed at providing a forum for Catholic parishioners who grieve the loss of their parish community. The ultimate question for this book is: How can any parish community continue to preserve its viability while going through the significant changes associated with merging, closing and collaborating models of parish life?

The main subject of this book continues to be a focal point in the lives of many parish communities in the United States. The majority of parishes affected by various reconfiguration plans occurred largely in the Mid-West and the North-East Dioceses in the United States. However, the declining number of priests and priestly vocations, the shift in the demographics concerning the Catholic population in the United States, as well as the aging of the "die-hard" generation of Catholics, seem to indicate the phenomena of merging, closing and collaborating of parishes is far from over. Most seminaries in the United States lack curriculum focused on the best and worst practices of parish reconfiguration. For that reason, the author of this book hopes to provide support and assistance to existing and future parish leaders and respective communities facing the challenges of a parish merger, closure and collaboration.

Ministerial Context and Rationale

The case study used for this book reflects the lives of nine ethnically and culturally diverse Catholic parishes from the Diocese of Youngstown, Ohio, which experienced the process of merging, closing and collaborating in recent years. The ministerial context of this book is based on their history and challenges which they experienced first-hand. These nine Catholic parishes have been the places where "God encounters God's people,"[2] and where the Catholic faithful immerse themselves in their ethnic culture, symbols and traditions. In some cases, their sacred grounds are now being used for secular purposes. The author of this book tends to believe that while some mergers and closures have been successful, others ended up in failure creating unnecessary divisions and hurt feelings. The author of this book intends to emphasize the best and the worst practices used in regard to the issue at hand based on the examples of nine parishes from the Diocese of Youngstown, Ohio. Each parish reflects a different aspect of the main subject of this book. The names of parishioners and pastors used in this book have been omitted in order to protect the identity of survey participants, their privacy, and to present an objective and accurate ministerial setting for the book. Each one of the three sets of parishes used for this study will reveal the historical background of the parishes, reasons for the closure, merger or collaboration and the input and reflections from the pastors, members of the parish staff and selected representatives of each parish community.

---

[2] Tim Sensing, *Qualitative Research: A-Multi Method Approach to Books for Doctor of Ministry Theses* (Eugene, Oregon: Wipf and Stock, 2011), 13.

Preliminary Book Assumptions

The preliminary assumption of the author of this book is that with the involvement of transparency, frequent communication and open dialogue in the process of closing, merging or collaboration of parishes, there is a greater chance of success. Many authors who had written books and articles regarding this subject emphasize that change in general - any change, whether it is positive or negative - is always treated with suspicion and fear. Closing a parish or proposing a merger/collaboration model may cause much anxiety and fear of the unknown in the lives of the faithful and parish leaders involved in this endeavor. Some people deal with a merger or closure of their parish church the same way they deal with the reality of death. Gerald A. Arbuckle reiterated this undeniable truth when he said;

> Today when hospitals, schools or churches close, or when there are liturgical changes, even if the reasons are sound, there are often vociferous protests from affected people. No amount of logical argument will convince them that the closures are in their best interests. One significant factor behind these outcries is the hidden function of these institutions: they ritually exist to contain people's fear of death. Their closure reminds people that death is a reality.[3]

When parishes merge, close or enter into collaboration, all parties involved in the process are faced with the impending need for a change that either may become life giving or life ending. Some people may argue that it is all about a matter of perspective, while others may be convinced that it has everything to do with the preconceived notions of what it means to be a member of a parish church community. Whatever the case may be, the author of this book dares to argue that any serious change in the life of a local parish church requires transparency, frequent communication and open dialogue. The basis of the author's assumption described above comes from the available theological and non-theological literature as well as the consultation with other pastors, parishioners, and the author's personal experience. When appropriately explained and timely executed, mergers, closures or collaborative models of parish life and existence can either breathe new life into the parish community in transition or take the remaining signs of life away. Parish leaders and parishioners who have experienced such transitions as active members of a church community emphasize the importance of ongoing and open dialogue between the diocesan representatives and the affiliates of the parish community in transition. Many authors who have written extensively on this subject seem to emphasize that if there is no dialogue with the parishioners and the decision of closure or merger is presented as a "top-down" management decision forced upon the parishioners, such process will undoubtedly fail. Consultation, honesty, and openness

---

[3] Arbuckle, Gerald A. *Culture, Inculturation, and Theologians: A Postmodern Critique.* (Collegeville, MN: Liturgical Press, 2010), 85.

to compromise, are fundamental elements of this process, and they should never be disregarded or ignored by all parties involved. All people involved in this process whether they are diocesan representatives, pastors, parish staff members or parishioners must be treated with the same respect and dignity. Ordained or non-ordained, all parties involved in this process must be presented with a forum to express their opinions and feelings, and they need to be assured that their voices and opinions count. Pastoral sensitivity, especially in the planning phase of the process and its actual implementation must always be a guiding principal in this enterprise. Fr. Robert Howes, a priest from the Diocese of Joliet, IL who had written a book called *Bridges: Toward the Inter-Parish Regional Community....Deaneries, Clusters, Plural Parishes.*, based on his thirty years of experience regarding parish planning and reconfigurations, made the following observation: "Other parishes agreed with their assessment that parishes should not be closed from the top down, but from the bottom up, adding that slipping attendance and decreasing financial support should be among the criteria a parish itself uses in determining its viability."[4]

Theological and Theoretical Foundations

It would be impossible to provide some pastoral recommendation for parish communities that want to remain vibrant while going through a merger, closure or collaboration process without first providing a solid theological and theoretical base for such a plan. The theological portion of this book will reflect on several essential elements which constitute the foundation of a church community. The author of this book intends to provide answers to the following questions: What is the mission of the Church and parish communities? What makes a parish community viable? What are the parish rights and obligations and who can claim them? What are the key elements involved in parish mergers, closures, and collaborations? What are the requirements of Canon Law referring to parish structural changes? How does the canonical process work for parish closures and mergers? The questions mentioned above will be answered in a systematic order using Scripture references, Church history, the teachings of the Magisterium expressed by the Vatican II Council and various theologians as well as the teachings of the recent popes. The main idea behind this approach is to present the history and theology of a parish church and its relationship with a diocese and the Universal Church. The theoretical part of this book will also provide a deeper understanding of the Canon Law's perspective regarding the closing and merging of parishes. Moreover, particular attention will be given to the canonical process for merging and closing of parishes and the authority of a local bishop "to erect, suppress or alter parishes." (canon 515, §2) In particular, the author wishes to discuss the specific criteria and requirements necessary for the process of closing and merging of parishes to be valid in light of Canon Law. The role of different parties involved in the process of a successful merger, closure or collaboration will also be also presented in order to emphasize the recommended and the discouraged practices.

---

[4] Howes, Robert G. *Bridges: Towards the Inter-Parish Regional Community...Deaneries, Clusters, Plural Parishes.* (Collegeville, MN: Liturgical Press, 1998), 46.

The Methodology of the Book

In order to achieve the aims and goals of this book, the author of this thesis will interview the pastors of the three case study parishes. In addition, parish staff members and selected parishioners will be asked to answer a survey developed by the author of this book. All participants involved will be assured of their right to privacy and confidentiality. The names of all participants will be kept anonymous and may be changed to protect their identity. However, all other data pertinent to the main subject of this book will be presented in the most accurate and transparent way possible. The nine parishes from the Diocese of Youngstown have been selected for this study because of their culturally, historically and ethnically diverse parish situations. These nine parishes have been divided by the author of this book into three sets based on their geographical location. The first set from Newton Falls reflects the merging of two parishes into one unit and eventually closing one of them. The second set from Warren presents the merging of three parishes into one single unit. The third set from Campbell is an example of merger and collaboration between four diverse ethnic parishes under the leadership of one pastor and initially one associate pastor whose ministry evolved around three different worship sites.

The first above mentioned set of parishes is very close to the author's heart as he took upon himself the challenge of merging the Polish and Slovak parish communities into one single-parish unit. Although it was one of the most painful experiences in his priestly ministry, he had no other choice but to close the Polish parish. The information obtained from the personal interviews and questionnaire will be described in detail in order to provide the most accurate context of the pastoral situation in question. Each of the three sets of parishes, their history, struggles, challenges, and hopes and dreams for the future will be presented in this case study. The author of this book intends to organize obtained data and present it in the form of various charts and tables. This data will reflect people's attitudes and understanding of what it means to be a viable parish community and what role the church community plays in the process of merging, closing or collaborating with other parishes.

Anticipated Outcomes

In the final chapter of this book, the author will provide a pastoral reflection concerning the recommended practices in the process of merging, closing or creating collaborative parish units. In addition, elements requiring pastoral sensitivity and attention will be emphasized. Pastoral reflection based on the survey data and various elements of the process will be presented in order to assist parish leaders and parishioners as they oversee and participate in the process of merging, closing or creating collaborative parish units. The author of this book hopes that by using his own experience of merging and eventually closing one of his former parishes, he will be able to raise pastoral sensitivity and deepen the awareness of the subject at hand. The advice and insights offered by the pastors involved in this case study will also be summarized and presented.

The author of this book sincerely hopes that by sharing his research, data and reflections from parish leaders, parish staff, and parishioners, this undertaking will help all parties involved to find and develop the most successful plan of action for their own diverse ministerial setting. Lastly, these pastoral recommendations are intended to serve as a helpful tool for the seasoned pastors as well as the newly appointed pastors who are making their first steps at creating a viable parish community in these fast paced and ever changing times. Recent statistics regarding the declining numbers of priests and the growing number of parishes without a resident pastor seem to indicate that the phenomenon of closing, merging and creating of collaborative parish units is far from over. The need to address this phenomenon and to provide some practical pastoral advice for all parties involved in this process seems to be even more dire than ever before.

CHAPTER II.

THEORETICAL OVERVIEW AND THEOLOGICAL GROUNDING

What is a Parish and How Did it Come to Exist?

Definition and Short History of Parish Development

Most postmodern Catholics and non-Catholics are familiar with the term *parish* when someone is referring to a local Catholic Church community as a point of reference. For the majority of the Roman Catholics living around the world and numbering 1.2 billion strong,[5] their first and most intimate experience of the Catholic Church takes place at a local parish. Their local parish church community is where they discover and nurture their call to discipleship. A local parish is a sacred place where Catholics experience God's love and compassion through the reception of the sacraments. It is a community of the Church. The word church derives from the Greek: *ekklesia* and the Latin: *ecclesia*. It indicates a community of those who have been called out by the Lord Jesus. It is a community called to go forth into the world and spread the message of the Gospel. As James A. Coriden eloquently stated: "*Ekklesia* most commonly referred to the town meetings or voting assemblies of the free citizens of Greek and Roman cities. The Greek word *ekklesia* had been used to translate the expression 'assembly of God' or 'those called together by God' (*qahal YHWH*) in the Hebrew scriptures when those scriptures were translated into Greek in Alexandria more than two centuries before Christ."[6]

Many current parish members belonging to the Greatest Generation, the Baby Boomer Generation and even the X and Y Generations consider their local parish to be a sacred ground where its diverse members enter into a relationship with God and with one another. It is to a certain degree an oasis of peace and tranquility where the parishioners realize and carry out their call to discipleship. It is a very special place where members of a church community follow their call to the ministry of service by caring each other's burdens. Burdens are carried by promoting unity among diverse church members and by encouraging and expressing solidarity with one another and with all those who call themselves Christians.

The word *parish* derives from the Greek noun *parokia* that can be understood as "those who lived close by one another, or it could mean those who were sojourners in an alien land, diaspora communities amidst pagan neighbors."[7] As Christianity continued to spread through the missionary efforts of the apostles and their disciples,

---

[5] Vatican Information Service; Holy See Press Office: *Presentation of Pontifical Yearbook 2013,* (May 13, 2013), Vatican, https://romancatholicworld.files.wordpress.com/2013/05/vis-news-holy-see-press-office-presentation-of-pontifical-yearbook-2013.pdf (accessed October 19, 2015).

[6] James A. Coriden, *The Parish in Catholic Tradition: History, Theology, and Canon Law* (Mahwah, N.J: Paulist Press, 1997), 16.

[7] Eugene Duffy, "Clustering Parishes II: The Theology." *Furrow* 61 (June 2010): 354.

the word *parish* was commonly used in reference to individual early church communities. It is of particular importance to remember that the early church communities consisted of a relatively small number of members estimated by scholars to be between thirty and forty. Those early Christian assemblies often were referred to as house or household churches. When new converts to the Christian faith embraced Christ, it was more often than not a decision reflecting the disposition of the entire household. When the master of the house had converted to Christianity, other family members, close friends, servants, and slaves were expected to do the same.

Most early Christian communities were founded in the larger urban melting pots such as Jerusalem, Antioch, Corinth, Ephesus, Smyrna, Damascus, Alexandria, Carthage, Lyons, and Rome. Toward the end of the first century, the Gentile converts became the majority group in the early church. As Christianity continued to spread far and wide geographically, the followers of Jesus could be found in many cities throughout Asia Minor as well as the eastern Mediterranean. Peter Phan makes the following critical observation regarding the expansion of Christianity in the first four centuries:

> In fact, in the first four centuries, the most successful fields of mission were not Europe but West Asia and Africa, with Syria as the center of gravity of Christianity before 500. The most vibrant and influential Christian centers were found in Asian and African cities such as Damascus and Alexandria, Axum and Antioch (where, incidentally, the followers of Jesus first became known as Christians); and in countries such as Armenia (the first Christian nation), India, and somewhat later, in China. Of the five ancient patriarchates, only Rome was located in the West, and of the remaining four, three were found in Asia (Jerusalem, Antioch, and Constantinople) and one in Africa (Alexandria).[8]

As time went on the early church communities blended into the Greco-Roman society and adopted some of its traditions, protocols, and structures. The Edict of Milan in 313 AD made Christianity one of the official religions of the Roman Empire. However, not until seventy-eight years later in the year 391 did Christianity become the official religion of the empire by the edict of the Emperor Theodosius. Since the practice of Christianity was no longer penalized but rather encouraged on all levels of the Greco-Roman culture and societal structure, the numbers of new Christian converts grew rapidly. The early church communities were very welcoming and inclusive. Indeed, they welcomed all who accepted Christ and who wanted to be members of the church (Acts 10-11, 15; Gal 2).

As Christianity spread from the urban settings to the countryside and little towns, the early church was already in the process of adapting some of the structures existing in the Greco-Roman culture and governance. Both terms *ekklesia* (church) and *paroikia* (parish) have been used interchangeably in the New Testament while

---

[8] Peter Phan, "Speaking in Many Tongues: Why the Church Must Be More Catholic," *Commonweal* 134, no. 1 (January 12, 2007): 17-18.

describing the early church communities. Regarding leadership roles in the early church, it important to remember that parish priests did not exist until the second half of the fourth century. According to Jean Colson there were two distinct forms of early church organization and leadership at that time:

> The first is Paul's line, which has a college of presbyters (elders) but no bishop president. Unity is based not on a single leader but the theology of the body of Christ with many members and many distinct functions. These presbyterial communities (no bishop) survived long into post-apostolic times, especially in Alexandria, Egypt. The second form of community organization characterized is by a single leader, a monarchic bishop (literally, *an overseer*) who resides in the community. This leader is the living image of the unity of the community. After the apostolic period, this monarchical community (one bishop) emerges as the dominant form of church organization.[9]

It is worth noting that the early church leaders were chosen, recognized and accepted by the local church community and its elders. A leader of the community was selected to preside over the Eucharist, to teach, to preach and if necessary to admonish the community. The selected leader was considered to have an apostolic succession since the leader was chosen by members of a community that had been founded and/or built upon the teachings of the apostles. With the passing of time the specialized ministers or groups of ministers called "orders" came into existence and were commonly accepted by various Christian communities. Some modern day scholars point out the existence of the following ministers in the early church: prophets, deacons, deaconesses, overseers, episkopos, presbyterous, leitourgos, neoteros and others.[10] Bishops (Greek *episkopoi* – meaning "overseers") resided in urban areas and they had numerous helpers who served in the capacity of priests (Greek *presbyteroi* – meaning "elders"), deacons (Greek *diakonoi* – meaning "servants" and deaconesses (διάκονοι γυναῖκες –"deacon women," who ministered to the various needs of the community. Eventually, priests and deacons were assigned by a bishop to different city districts to serve the people entrusted to their pastoral care. Presbyters were also sent to minister to the new converts who lived outside of the city limits in remote villages and rural areas. Soon the people residing in the countryside were cared for by a "rural bishop," also known as *chorepiscopoi* who were at times referred to as *corepiscopoi* – "country bishops."[11] Eventually the country bishops fell under the jurisdiction of a city bishop.

---

[9] William J. Rademacher, John Weber S., and David McNeill, *Understanding Today's Catholic Parish* (New London, CT: Twenty-Third Publications, 2007), 8.

[10] Kennan Osborne, *Priesthood* (New York and Mahwah, New Jersey: Paulist Press, 1980), 42-44.

[11] James A. Coriden, *The Parish in Catholic Tradition: History, Theology, and Canon Law* (Mahwah, N.J: Paulist Press, 1997), 23.

By the beginning of the fifth century, the rural bishops were replaced by priests. The priests, in most cases, were better educated and more equipped to lead a Christian community of the faithful. Those presbyters were the delegates of a city bishop who alone had the authority to ordain priests and appoint them as officially recognized ministers of the Gospel and leaders of a community. Priests were representatives of a bishop, and they were allowed to preside over the Eucharistic celebration in the absence of a bishop.

After the death of Emperor Constantine in 337, the Church had adapted to its own organizational structure the Roman system of regional districts called "dioceses."[12] Terms such as the Greek *parokia,* meaning "parish," (Latin: *paroecia*) and the word "diocese" from the Latin, *dioecesis,* and its Greek equivalent, διοίκησις, meaning "administration," have been used interchangeably for some time to refer to the same district or a region. With the passing of time, diocesan and local churches became recognized by Roman Law as "a public juridic person" with a right to own property. Some of the churches gained the status of baptismal churches. Those were the churches especially designated for the celebration of baptisms which initially were reserved for the bishop; others were privately owned proprietary churches and still others became titular churches dedicated to a particular patron or a founder.

As time went on and certain locations became associated with local congregations, they were named or titled after martyrs or other renowned Christians. Some of these buildings became dedicated to the uses of the community and came into the possession of the community. There were twenty such 'titular churches' in Rome in the first half of the third century. Each of the titular churches was served by a presbyter or two, and perhaps a deacon. They were quite consciously in communion with the bishop of the city or town. For example, they sometimes received the eucharistic bread (*fermentum*) sent to them from the bishop's own celebration of the Lord's Supper as a sign of that communion. The titular churches were more personal than territorial, that is, they were not geographical subdivisions of the larger urban or regional church but simply congregations to which the faithful belonged. In other words, the titular churches of the third and fourth centuries were not parishes in our contemporary sense, but they were one of the forerunners of what later were called parishes.[13]

As Christianity continued to spread, more priests were ordained and assigned to lead a variety of congregations who lived outside the city limits. The growth in numbers of local church communities under the guidance of a pastor-presbyter, who answered to a city bishop, was slowly becoming the norm for the organizational

---

[12] William J. Rademacher, John Weber S., and David McNeill, *Understanding Today's Catholic Parish* (New London, CT: Twenty-Third Publications, 2007), 11.

[13] James A. Coriden, *The Parish in Catholic Tradition: History, Theology, and Canon Law* (Mahwah, N.J: Paulist Press, 1997), 21.

structure of the early church. However, as some scholars point out, it is imperative to remember that the early Christian church communities were not bound by the limits of their geographic territory.

Within this incredible variety of church organization, only three principles emerge with any consistency. First, territory or property with boundaries is not the determining factor in defining the local church. Second, the rural priest always remains the delegate of the city bishop. He comes from the bishop's altar and is responsible to him. This remains true even when priests are appointed to different regions of the city. Third, the priest does not ordain other priests. In the Western church, he does not perform the chrismation (the anointing with chrism) even when, in the absence of the bishop, he begins to administer baptism. Thus, chrismation, or confirmation, is gradually separated from baptism.[14]

After the second invasion of Rome by the Vandals in 455 and the fall of the Western Roman Empire in 476, Western Europe embraced feudalism as a new system of social order.

The traditional date, designated by historian Edward Gibbon, for the fall of Rome is A.D. 476, when the Germanic chieftain Odoacer, himself a Roman general, marched on Italy and captured Rome. He then turned on Ravenna, where he deposed the teenage emperor Romulus Augustus on September 4, 476, and declared himself king. As the first Germanic king of Italy and the Western Empire, his sword-backed coronation makes for a convenient end date.[15]

The nobility with the right to own land provided military support for the King and the Crown. Noble Lords often leased or bequeathed portions of their land to various vassals who in turn provided employment and military protection for the peasants. From the fifth to the sixth century, the feudal system was in place as a response to the chaos and fragmentation that followed the demise of the Western Roman Empire. The Church and the Christian faithful were also influenced by this new system of social structure and organization. At the start of the eighth-century the number of churches privately funded, owned and operated by noble lords grew significantly. Affluent and financially independent lords and nobility built churches on their grounds. They then would employ a priest by providing him with room, board and financial compensation for services rendered. A portion of the priest's income also came from the stole fees for the administration of the sacraments and from the church grounds. Since a parish priest was considered to be a vassal of the

---

[14] William J. Rademacher, John Weber S., and David McNeill, *Understanding Today's Catholic Parish* (New London, CT: Twenty-Third Publications, 2007), 10.

[15] Michael S. Malone, *The Guardian of All Things: The Epic Story of Human Memory* (New York, NY: St. Martin's Press, 2012), 82.

landlord, it was at the discretion of the noble lord to employ or to remove a priest from the local church. Charlemagne, King of the Franks and the Holy Roman Emperor (786-814), returned the control of the local churches back to the bishops. Bishops had the final say in the matters considering priest appointments and maintenance of a church. Interestingly, the removal of a priest from a parish fell not under the authority of a bishop or a landlord but rather to a church court.

As a result of proprietary structures, a significant inversion occurred in the way that local congregations were officially viewed. Legally, parishes became characterized as pastoral offices that provided support for the clergy rather than communities for the spiritual welfare of the faithful. It seems almost incredible in retrospect, but for several centuries parishes were defined as benefices. A benefice is a sacred office, like that of a pastor, to which is connected the permanent right to receive income from the endowment attached to the office. In the church's juridical order, from the twelfth century until the Code revision of 1983, a parish was looked upon as a spiritual reality (the pastoral office) with a temporal reality (the endowment or other income source) united in one institution: a benefice, that is, an office with a reliable income source for the officeholder.[16]

The industrial revolution from the late eighteenth through the nineteenth centuries had a tremendous impact on the life of the church both local and universal. The shifts in demographics of the faithful, the continuous migration of people from rural areas to urban centers and an ongoing secularization of society had a tremendous influence on parish life both in large cities and small villages. This concept of a territorial parish confined to its geographical location changed dramatically after the Second Vatican Council (1962-1965). The local parish church was once again seen as a community of people who were unified by their faith and defined by Canon Law as "a definitive community of Christian faithful established on a stable basis within a particular church" (canon 515, §1). James H. Provost made a crucial observation regarding this subject: "Once established, this community of the faithful has the right to permanent existence; it is a public juridic person (canon 515, §3) which by its nature is perpetual (canon 120, §1)."[17]

The Theology of a Local Parish Church in the Teachings of the Vatican II Council and Beyond.

Vatican II Council (1962-1965)

On October 11, 1962, the eve of the Vatican II Council, Pope St. John XXIII presented his vision for the Catholic Church in his opening remarks, and many

---

[16] James A. Coriden, *The Parish in Catholic Tradition: History, Theology, and Canon Law* (Mahwah, N.J: Paulist Press, 1997), 28.

[17] James H. Provost, "Some Canonical Considerations On Closing Parishes," *Jurist* 53 (February 1993): 363.

Catholics and non-Catholics sensed that a great transformation was on its way. Indeed, the teachings of the Vatican II Council and the implementation of its reforms brought a monumental change in the life of the Church. Some fifty years later present day Catholics can still feel the impact of the Vatican II Council on Catholic theology, the Institutional Church and the Catholic faithful. The more visible changes took place in regards to Catholic worship (norms concerning the worship environment) and the Official Liturgy of the Church (the way Eucharist was to be celebrated). The celebration of the Eucharist was to take place in the vernacular language of the worshipping community instead of Latin. The presider of the Mass was no longer separated from the rest of the congregation by communion railings which divided the sanctuary area (also called the presbyterium) from the remainder of the church. The main altar for the celebration of the Eucharist was moved forward, closer to the people so that they could see and feel a stronger connection with the sacred mysteries that were being celebrated. Also, the presider was no longer saying the mass with his back to the congregation. With the reforms of the Vatican II Council, the presider was facing the people while celebrating the sacred liturgy. The Catholic faithful were encouraged to sing and to exchange the sign of peace during the Eucharistic celebration. Considering that no major reforms of the Church's liturgy had been introduced since the Council of Trent (1545-1563), the teachings of the Vatican II Council were perceived by some in the Church as revolutionary. The Vatican II Council inspired much-needed change in the liturgy as well as in the life of the Church.

Through study of various Vatican II Council documents, especially *Lumen Gentium* of November 21, 1964 [The Dogmatic Constitution on the Church],[18] it becomes self-evident that the council fathers introduced a momentous shift in terminology and theology concerning the lay faithful and their role in the Church, both local and universal. Instead of being perceived as passive recipients of the sacraments, the people in the pews were encouraged to become fully engaged in the celebrated mysteries. *Sacrosanctum Concilium* of December 4, 1963, [The Constitution on the Sacred Liturgy], no. 14, makes this important point by stating that:

> Mother Church earnestly desires that all the faithful should be led to that fully conscious, and active participation in liturgical celebrations which is demanded by the very nature of the liturgy. Such participation by the Christian people as 'a chosen race, a royal priesthood, a holy nation, a redeemed people (1 Pet. 2:9; cf. 2:4-5), is their right and duty by reason of their baptism.' In the restoration and promotion of the sacred liturgy, this full and active participation by all the people is the aim to be considered before all else; for it is the primary and indispensable source from which the faithful are

---

[18] Second Vatican Ecumenical Council. The Dogmatic Constitution on the Church *Lumen Gentium*, (November 21, 1964), Vatican, http://www.vatican.va/archive/hist_councils/ii_vatican_council/ documents/vat - ii_const_19641121_lumen-gentium_en.html (accessed January 18, 2016). Here after cited as *Lumen Gentium*.

to derive the true Christian spirit; and therefore pastors of souls must zealously strive to achieve it, by means of the necessary instruction, in all their pastoral work.[19]

In addition, the council fathers underlined the importance of lay involvement in the life of the Church and the world in which they live and function. The council fathers purposely placed Chapter II, "The People of God," of *Lumen Gentium* before Chapter III, "The Hierarchical Structure of the Church." In doing so, the council fathers signaled a shift from the highly clerical and hierarchical structure of the Catholic Church to a restored role and voice of the Catholic faithful in the life of the Church and the matters pertaining to her role and mission in the world. The terminology used previously in regards to the lay faithful was also changed. The Vatican II Council clarified the role of the faithful in the life of the Church and the world. The term "lay people," had been used in the past history of the Church as a way of describing those who were not a part of the priestly order. This term has often been used to describe the non-ordained members of the Church, who were considered to be subordinate to the ordained hierarchy. However, with the teachings of the Vatican II Council, the term "lay faithful or laity," is being used and presented in a more positive way. The various documents of the Vatican II Council refer to the laity as "the People of God,"[20] "God's people,"[21] "members of the Mystical Body of Christ,"[22] "sharers and co-workers,"[23] and "witnesses of Christ."[24] The council fathers defined the role of the laity in the Church and thus opened the doors of the Church to them by encouraging the faithful to get involved in the life and mission of the Church.

In regard to the theology of a local church, and parish life and ministry in particular, a significant shift in terminology, as well as ecclesiology of a local church

---

[19] Second Vatican Ecumenical Council. The Constitution on the Sacred Liturgy *Sacrosanctum Concilium,* (December 4, 1963), 14, Vatican, http://www.vatican.va/archive/hist_councils/ii_vatican_council/documents/vat-ii_const_19631204_sacrosanctum-concilium_en.html (accessed January 18, 2016). Here after cited as *Sacrosanctum Concilium.*

[20] *Lumen Gentium,* 9, 11, 12, 32.

[21] Second Vatican Ecumenical Council. Pastoral Constitution on the Church in the Modern World *Gaudium et Spes,* (December 7, 1965), 3, Vatican ,http://www.vatican.va/archive/hist_councils/ii_vatican _council/documents/vat-ii_const_19651207_gaudium-et-spes_en.htm (accessed January 19, 2016). Here after cited as *Gaudium et Spes.*

[22] Second Vatican Ecumenical Council. Decree on the Apostolate of Lay People *Apostolicam Actuositatem,* (November 18, 1965), 2, 3, Vatican, http://www.vatican.va/archive/hist_councils/ii_vatican_council/documents/ vatii_decree_19651118_apostolicam-actuositatem_en.html (accessed January 19, 2016). Here after cited as *Apostolicam Actuositatem.*

[23] *Apostolicam Actuositatem,* 10, 33.

[24] *Lumen Gentium,* 10.

community, has taken place. No longer was the local parish referred to only in terms of a geographically designated territory for worship as it had been the case in the past history. In the 1917 Code of Canon Law a parish was defined as: "a distinct territorial part of the diocese (*distincta pars territorialis)* with its proper church, people, and rector as its proper pastor."[25] (canon 216, § 1, 3) The teachings of Vatican II Council shifted the understanding of a local parish from a distinct territory to the People of God, a community of the faithful united through the Eucharist and living in accordance with the Gospel. This point has been made indirectly in the Decree on the Pastoral Office of Bishops in the Church:

> A diocese is a portion of the people of God which is entrusted to a bishop to be shepherded by him with the cooperation of the presbytery. Thus by adhering to its pastor and gathered together by him through the Gospel and the Eucharist in the Holy Spirit, it constitutes a particular church in which the one, holy, Catholic, and apostolic Church of Christ is truly present and operative.[26]

The People of God, the laity, share in the three *munera Christi* (three offices or functions of Christ) and the overall mission of the Church;

> These faithful are by baptism made one body with Christ and are constituted among the People of God; they are in their own way made sharers in the priestly, prophetical, and kingly functions of Christ; and they carry out for their own part the mission of the whole Christian people in the Church and in the world.[27]

They have been called by the Lord Jesus to bear witness and to get involved in the temporal affairs of the world following the teachings of the Gospel and seeking the Kingdom of God. What became apparent from the teachings of the Vatican II Council was the notion that every baptized member of the Church has an important task and role in the Church. Each member has been called by God to make the Kingdom of God present in his/her midst through her/his particular vocation and God's given gifts and talents. By virtue of baptism, the People of God become members of the Church and they share in the responsibility to proclaim the Gospel of Christ to all corners of the world, to evangelize and to make the Kingdom of God present in our midst. The Dogmatic Constitution on the Church makes this point in paragraph 12 by stating:

---

[25] John P. Beal, James A. Coriden, and Thomas J. Green, eds. *New Commentary on the Code of Canon Law* (Mahwah, NJ: Paulist Press, 2010), 689.

[26] Second Vatican Ecumenical Council. Decree on the Pastoral Office of Bishops in the Church *Christus Dominus,* (October 28, 1965), 11, Vatican, http://www.vatican.va/archive/hist_councils/ii_vatican_council/ documents/vat-ii_decree_19651028_christus-dominus_en.html (accessed January 19, 2016). Here after cited as *Christus Dominus.*

[27] *Lumen Gentium,* 31.

The holy people of God share also in Christ's prophetic office; it spreads abroad a living witness to Him, especially by means of a life of faith and charity and by offering to God a sacrifice of praise, the tribute of lips which give praise to His name (Hebr. 13:15).[28]

Later in the same paragraph the council fathers reminded all members of the Church that:

It is not only through the sacraments and the ministries of the Church that the Holy Spirit sanctifies and leads the people of God and enriches it with virtues, but, allotting his gifts to everyone according as He wills (1 Cor. 12:11)… He distributes special graces among the faithful of every rank. By these gifts He makes them fit and ready to undertake the various tasks and offices which contribute toward the renewal and building up of the Church, according to the words of the Apostle: The manifestation of the Spirit is given to everyone for profit (1 Cor. 12:7)… These charisms, whether they be the more outstanding or, the more simple and widely diffused, are to be received with thanksgiving and consolation for they are perfectly suited to and useful for the needs of the Church.[29]

All members of the Church have been empowered by the gifts of the Holy Spirit for various ministries in the Church and they are called to "become good stewards of God's varied grace (1 Pt. 4:10)." Each church member is called to build up the Church – the body of Christ. Although we may have different gifts and functions in the Body of Christ, nevertheless each part of the body has a significant role to contribute to the wellbeing of the entire Body of Christ – the Church. St. Paul, the Apostle to the Gentiles, emphasized this point in his letter to the Romans;

Since we have gifts that differ according to the grace given to us, let us exercise them: if prophecy, in proportion to the faith; if ministry, in ministering; if one is a teacher, in teaching; if one exhorts, in exhortation; if one contributes, in generosity; if one is over others, with diligence; if one does acts of mercy, with cheerfulness.[30]

All gifts are to be exercised for the benefit of the entire community. Moreover, the guiding principle for all Church members in everything they say and do should be love; "So faith, hope, love remain, these three; but the greatest of these is love."[31] All members of the community of faith must support the entire body

---

[28] *Lumen Gentium,* 12.

[29] Ibid.

[30] Rom. 12:6-8.

[31] 1 Cor. 13:13.

formed by all believers with Christ as its head; "living the truth in love, we should grow in every way into him who is the head, Christ, from whom the whole body, joined and held together by every supporting ligament, with the proper functioning of each part, brings about the body's growth and builds itself up in love."[32] Members of Christ's Church are citizens of two cities, two realms, two worlds (Hebr. 13:14). The council fathers underlined this point by stating; "The council exhorts Christians, as citizens of both cities, to perform their duties faithfully in the spirit of the gospel....(they) have here no lasting city, but seek the city which is to come."[33]

While they live, here and now, their eyes also need to be fixed on the Kingdom of Heaven that is yet to come with its full realization at the end of time. Church members are called to permeate the light of the Gospel into the secular spheres of their lives. They are to infuse the Gospel in their homes, families, workplaces, cultures and everywhere else where they are engaged in their earthly duties. They have been given a particular vocation to share in the mission of the Church and to evangelize the world.

The lay apostolate, however, is a participation in the salvific mission of the Church itself. Through their baptism and confirmation, all are commissioned to that apostolate by the Lord Himself. Moreover, by the sacraments, especially holy Eucharist, that charity toward God and man which is the soul of the apostolate is communicated and nourished. Now the laity are called in a special way to make the Church present and operative in those places and circumstances where only through them can it become the salt of the earth. Thus every layman, in virtue of the very gifts bestowed upon him, is at the same time a witness and a living instrument of the mission of the Church itself according to the measure of Christ's bestowal.[34]

Lay members of the Church have a specific role as co-workers in the vineyard of the Lord to participate in the mission of the Church aimed at the salvation of the entire human race. The council fathers underlined that dimension of their vocation by encouraging them to become active participants in the mission of salvation: "The laity are called to participate actively in the entire life of the church; not only are they to animate the world with the spirit of Christianity, they are to be witnesses to Christ in all circumstances and at the very heart of the human community."[35] Through their active involvement in the mission of the Church, the lay faithful share in the vast responsibility of making the Church the universal sacrament of salvation:

---

[32] Eph. 4:15-16.

[33] *Gaudium et Spes,* 42.

[34] *Lumen Gentium,* 33.

[35] *Gaudium et Spes,* 43.

Whether it aids the world or whether it benefits from it, the church has but one sole purpose - that the kingdom of God may come and the salvation of the human race may be accomplished. Every benefit the people of God can confer on humanity during its earthly pilgrimage is rooted in the church's being 'the universal sacrament of salvation,' at once manifesting and actualizing the mystery of God's love for humanity.[36]

The primary mission of Church members engaged in the life of their local and universal Church is to proclaim Christ and to transform the temporal order of the world in the spirit of the Gospel.[37] The lay apostolate is called to become a community of active agents in the process of evangelization. They have been called by Christ to lead others to the faith by their words, deeds, and actions. This call to new evangelization is an important part of their vocation:

Christ's redemptive work, while essentially concerned with the salvation of men, includes also the renewal of the whole temporal order. Hence, the mission of the Church is not only to bring the message and grace of Christ to men but also to penetrate and perfect the temporal order with the spirit of the Gospel. In fulfilling this mission of the Church, the Christian laity exercise their apostolate both in the Church and in the world, in both the spiritual and the temporal orders. These orders, although distinct, are so connected in the singular plan of God that He Himself intends to raise up the whole world again in Christ and to make it a new creation, initially on earth and completely on the last day. In both orders the layman, being simultaneously a believer and a citizen, should be continuously led by the same Christian conscience.[38]

While the lay faithful are not of this world and yet they live in the world, theirs is a particular task to evangelize and to grow in holiness as members of Christ's Body – the Church. "Therefore all in the Church, whether they belong to the hierarchy or are cared for by it, are called to holiness, according to the apostle's saying: for this is the will of God, your sanctification."[39] Evangelization and sanctification of oneself and others are fundamental parts of our Christian identity and the Church's mission in the world. As sharers in the mission of the Church, the involvement of lay people in their respective church communities is indispensable and absolutely necessary for evangelization efforts to be effective. "They should be so involved in the local community of the parish that they will acquire a consciousness of being living and active members of the people of God."[40] In a very

---

[36] Ibid., 45.

[37] *Lumen Gentium*, 33.

[38] *Apostolicam Actuositatem*, 5.

[39] *Lumen Gentium*, 39.

[40] *Apostolicam Actuositatem*, 30.

unique way, the lay faithful compliment the evangelization attempts of their pastors and fellow church members. More specifically, the lay apostolate and their activity "is so necessary within the Church communities that without it the apostolate of the pastors is often unable to achieve its full effectiveness."[41] Their involvement in the life of the Church must always be aimed at the benefit of the entire church community. Local parish churches are perfect platforms for lay participation and evangelization efforts aimed at the salvation of all God's children. In the words of *Apostolicam Actuositatem:*

> The parish offers an obvious example of the apostolate on the community level inasmuch as it brings together the many human differences within its boundaries and merges them into the universality of the Church. The laity should accustom themselves to working in the parish in union with their priests, bringing to the Church community their own and the world's problems as well as questions concerning human salvation, all of which they should examine and resolve by deliberating in common. As far as possible the laity ought to provide helpful collaboration for every apostolic and missionary undertaking sponsored by their local parish.[42]

As sharers in the mission to evangelize and to spread the message of the Gospel to all corners of the world, the lay apostolate are called to work collaboratively with other members of the Church (lay and ordained) in order to address the human and Christian needs of all who seek God and who wish to be saved.

> The faithful are called to engage in the apostolate as individuals in the varying circumstances of their life… For this reason, the faithful should participate in the apostolate by way of united effort. They should be apostles both in their family communities and in their parishes and dioceses, which themselves express the community nature of the apostolate, as well as in the informal groups which they decide to form among themselves.[43]

However, in order for the lay apostolate and their involvement in the life of the local and universal Church to be most effective, the council fathers called for an ongoing formation of lay faithful based on the church doctrine and the common call to live our lives as evangelical witnesses. "In regard to the apostolate for evangelizing and sanctifying men, the laity must be specially formed to engage in conversation with others, believers, or non-believers, in order to manifest Christ's message to all men."[44] Continuing education and formation of intentional disciples are indispensable

---

[41] Ibid., 10.

[42] Ibid.

[43] *Apostolicam Actuositatem,* 18.

elements in the process of New Evangelization. Laity's active involvement in the life of the church through the pursuit of personal sanctification and an authentic Christian witness are effective elements aimed at bringing into fulfillment the evangelizing mission of the church.

Papal Teachings Regarding the Local and the Universal Church and the Ongoing Need of Evangelization.

Pope Paul VI

Pope Paul VI reiterated the importance of evangelization on the local and universal levels of the Church's existence in his Apostolic Exhortation *Evangelii Nuntiandi*, (Proclaiming the Gospel). Published ten years after the conclusion of the Vatican II Council, this papal document emphasized the fundamental mission of the Church and her members, namely to evangelize and to become agents of the evangelization efforts in the world. Pope Paul VI understood evangelization not as a single act but rather as a rich, complex and dynamic process.[45] The Pastor of the Universal Church, Pope Paul VI, had placed evangelization at the very core of what it means to be the Church founded by Jesus Christ. Pope Paul VI defined evangelization in terms of: "proclaiming Christ to those who do not know Him, of preaching, of catechesis, of conferring Baptism and the other sacraments."[46] The call to evangelization in every time and place is one of the reasons for the Church's existence and an essential element of her identity:

> We wish to confirm once more that the task of evangelizing all people constitutes the essential mission of the Church. It is a task and mission which the vast and profound changes of present-day society make all the more urgent. Evangelizing is, in fact, the grace and vocation proper to the Church, her deepest identity. She exists in order to evangelize, that is to say, in order to preach and teach, to be the channel of the gift of grace, to reconcile sinners with God, and to perpetuate Christ's sacrifice in the Mass, which is the memorial of His death and glorious resurrection.[47]

For the Church to become an effective evangelizing agent in the world, she must allow herself to be evangelized in the first place. The Church needs to

---

[44] Ibid., 31.

[45] *Apostolicam Actuositatem,* 10.

[46] Paul VI, Apostolic ExhortationEvangelization in the Modern World *Evangelii Nuntiandi,* (December 8, 1975), 17, Vatican, http://w2.vatican. va/content/paul-vi/en/apost_exhortations/ documents/hf_p-vi_exh_19751208_ evangelii-nuntiandi.html (accessed January 19, 2016). Here after cited as *Evangelii Nuntiandi*.

[47] Ibid., 14.

evangelize herself by listening to the Word of God, by an ongoing renewal, and "it must constantly be on the road to conversion."[48] At the same time, she must also become an active promoter of evangelization in the world.

> Having been sent and evangelized, the Church herself sends out evangelizers. She puts on their lips the saving Word, she explains to them the message of which she herself is the depositary, she gives them the mandate which she herself has received and she sends them out to preach. To preach not their own selves or their personal ideas, but a Gospel of which neither she nor they are the absolute masters and owners, to dispose of it as they wish, but a Gospel of which they are the ministers, in order to pass it on with complete fidelity.[49]

The importance and engagement of a local parish church in the process of evangelization are unquestionable and imperative. One of the most useful tools in the evangelization efforts is an authentic witness given by individual Christians as well as by the church community. Pope Paul VI underlined the fact that modern people listen more attentively to witnesses rather than to teachers:

> For the Church, the first means of evangelization is the witness of an authentically Christian life, given over to God in a communion that nothing should destroy and at the same time given to one's neighbor with limitless zeal. As we said recently to a group of lay people, "Modern man listens more willingly to witnesses than to teachers, and if he does listen to teachers, it is because they are witnesses"…It is therefore primarily by her conduct and by her life that the Church will evangelize the world, in other words, by her living witness of fidelity to the Lord Jesus - the witness of poverty and detachment, of freedom in the face of the powers of this world, in short, the witness of sanctity.[50]

The importance of Christian witness and the need to re-evangelize the Catholic faithful living in the modern world has been emphasized by Pope John Paul II in his numerous writings on this subject including his weekly catechesis presented at the General Audience at St. Peter's Square at the Vatican.

---

[48] *Evangelii Nuntiandi*, 15.

[49] Ibid.

[50] Ibid., 41.

Saint Pope John Paul II

John Paul II has been called by some people the Great Communicator.[51] During the course of his twenty-eight years of service as the Vicar of Christ, the Polish Pope employed all kinds of communication tools, including the internet, in order to proclaim the Gospel of Christ and to foster evangelization efforts around the world. As the most traveled pontiff in over two thousand years of history of the Roman Catholic Church, John Paul II believed that evangelization is "the supreme duty" of every Christian and the entire Church.[52] The pope was convinced that the Church needs to engage the culture of the people to whom the Gospel of Christ is being proclaimed. At the same time, John Paul II is being credited as the author of the phrase, "New Evangelization."

> It is believed that Blessed John Paul II first used the term in 1983 in an address to Latin American Bishops. He would later bring this term to the attention of the entire Church. Perhaps, the most clear definition of the New Evangelization is in his encyclical, *Redemptoris Missio*. In section 33 of this encyclical, Blessed John Paul II describes three different situations for evangelization: mission *ad gentes*, Christian communities, and the new evangelization.[53]

In the course of his Petrine ministry, John Paul II realized that countries where Christianity has been present and alive for centuries were in a desperate need of New Evangelization. It became rather obvious to the new pope that some of the First World Countries have been steadily falling into secularism, materialism, individualism, and relativism. Five years after his election as the Pastor of the Universal Church, John Paul II addressed the Catholic Bishops of Latin America in Haiti in the following words: "The commemoration of the half millennium of evangelization will gain its full energy if it is a commitment, not to re-evangelize but to a New Evangelization, new in its ardor, methods and expression."[54] John Paul II encouraged all members of the Church to proclaim the Gospel of Christ in new ways

---

[51] John Paul II Foundation, November 4, 2013, Vatican, http://www.fjp2.com/en/news/vatican/ 19849-i-lived-with-a-saint-john-paul-iis-personal-secretary-releases-book-on-polish-pope (accessed October 20, 2015).

[52] John Paul II, Encyclical Letter On the Permanent Validity of the Church's Missionary Mandate *Redemptoris Missio,* (December 7, 1990), 3, Vatican, http://w2.vatican.va/content/john-paul-ii/en/ encyclicals/documents/hf_jp-ii_enc_07121990_redemptoris-missio.html (accessed January 19, 2016). Here after cited as *Redemptoris Missio*.

[53] The Fellowship of Catholic University Students *Focus* (June 3, 2013), Genesee, Colorado http://www.focus.org/blog/posts/what-is-the-new-evangelization.html (accessed January 13, 2016).

[54] John Paul II, Opening Address of the Nineteenth General Assembly of CELAM, (March 9, 1983), Port-au-Prince, Haiti, Printed in *L'Osservatore Romano* English Edition 16/780 (April 18, 1983), 9.

that can reach present culture and the people who live in it. Keenly aware of the ongoing secularism and religious indifference John Paul II emphasized the continuing need for the New Evangelization:

> Whole countries and nations where religion and the Christian life were formerly flourishing and capable of fostering a viable and working community of faith, are now put to a hard test, and in some cases, are even undergoing a radical transformation, as a result of a constant spreading of religious indifference, secularism and atheism. This particularly concerns countries and nations of the so-called First World, in which economic well-being and consumerism, even if coexistent with a tragic situation of poverty and misery, inspires and sustains a life lived 'as if God did not exist.'…In other regions or nations many vital traditions of piety and popular forms of Christian religion are still conserved; but today this moral and spiritual patrimony runs the risk of being dispersed under the impact of a multiplicity of processes, including secularization and the spread of sects. Only a re-evangelization can ensure the growth of a clear and deep faith, and serve to make these traditions a force for authentic freedom. Without doubt, a mending of the Christian fabric of society is urgently needed in all parts of the world. But for this to come about, what is needed is first to remake the Christian fabric of the ecclesial community itself present in these countries and nations.[55]

The New Evangelization ought to engage the current culture of the people of God and accompany them on their life and faith journey. John Paul II envisioned the process of the New Evangelization as a way of reaching out to those who have never heard about Christ, as well as those who are Christians and who need to heed the universal call to holiness and an ongoing conversion. Saint John Paul II also included those who "have lost a living sense of the faith, or even no longer consider themselves members of the Church, and live a life far removed from Christ and his Gospel. In this case what is needed is a "new evangelization."[56] John Paul II believed that the Church both local and universal should always consider itself as a missionary church. A missionary church is always involved in the process of evangelization where the Good News is being proclaimed in ways that reach the post-modern society. As a living presence of Christ in the world, the Church ought to evangelize and be evangelized at the same time. Local Christian communities, parishes, are capable of becoming signs of mature faith especially when they promote the universal call to become a missionary church.

[55] John Paul II, Post-Synodal Apostolic Exhortation On the Vocation and the Mission of the Lay Faithful in the Church and in the World *Christifideles Laici* (December 30, 1988), 34: *AAS* 81 (1989), 454-455. Also available online at http://w2.vatican.va/content/john-paul-ii/en/apost_exhortations/ documents/hf_jp-ii_exh_30121988_ christifideles-laici.html (accessed October 20, 2015). Here after cited as *Christifideles Laici*.

[56] *Redemptoris Missio*, 33.

There is still much to be done in implanting and developing the Church (in the modern world). Responsibility for this task belongs to the universal Church and to the particular churches, to the whole people of God and to all its missionary forces. Every church, even one made up of recent converts, is missionary by its very nature and is both evangelized and evangelizing. Faith must always be presented as a gift of God to be lived out in community (families, parishes, associations), and to be extended to others through witness in word and deed. The evangelizing activity of the Christian community, first in its own locality, and then elsewhere as part of the Church's universal mission, is the clearest sign of a mature faith. A radical conversion in thinking is required in order to become missionary, and this holds true both for individuals and entire communities. The Lord is always calling us to come out of ourselves and to share with others the goods we possess, starting with the most precious gift of all - our faith. The effectiveness of the Church's organizations, movements, parishes and apostolic works must be measured in the light of this missionary imperative. Only by becoming missionary will the Christian community be able to overcome its internal divisions and tensions, and rediscover its unity and its strength of faith.[57]

Faith is a gift from God that needs to grow and mature through an individual involvement in the life of various local church communities. The transmission of the faith through the efforts of the New Evangelization has been considered by John Paul II as a supreme duty of every believer and member of the Church. Saint John Paul II expressed this importance in his Apostolic Letter *Novo Millennio Ineunte* [On Entering the New Millennium, 2001]:

Over the years, I have often repeated the summons to the new evangelization. I do so again now, especially in order to insist that we must rekindle in ourselves the impetus of the beginnings and allow ourselves to be filled with the ardour of the apostolic preaching which followed Pentecost...This passion will not fail to stir in the Church a new sense of mission, which cannot be left to a group of 'specialists' but must involve the responsibility of all the members of the People of God. Those who have come into genuine contact with Christ cannot keep him for themselves, they must proclaim him. A new apostolic outreach is needed, which will be lived as the everyday commitment of Christian communities and groups. This should be done however with the respect due to the different paths of different people and with sensitivity to the diversity of cultures in which the Christian message must be planted, in such a way that the particular values of each people will not be rejected but purified and brought to their fullness.[58]

---

[57] *Redemptoris Missio*, 49.

[58] John Paul II, Apostolic Letter to the Bishops, Clergy and Lay Faithful at the Close of the Great Jubilee of 2000; At the Beginning of the New Millennium *Novo Millenio Ineunte*, (January 6, 2001), 40, Vatican, https://w2.vatican.va/content/john-paul-

Christians are called to dedicate themselves to the New Evangelization process based on the proclamation of Christ and his teachings with respect for the local customs and cultures where the Good News is being shared. The need for an authentic witness to the Gospel of Christ in the lives of church members and the universal call to holiness have been emphasized throughout John Paul II's Post-Synodal Apostolic Exhortation on the Vocation and Mission of the Lay Faithful in the Church and in the World, *Christifideles Laici* [The Lay Members of Christ's Faithful People], 1988. Here Saint John Paul II reminded all members of the Church about their universal call to holiness. Such holiness is necessary to bear witness to the Gospel of Christ in everything that the faithful do in the world and in the Church.

> We come to a full sense of the dignity of the lay faithful if we consider the prime and fundamental vocation that the Father assigns to each of them in Jesus Christ through the Holy Spirit: the vocation to holiness, that is, the perfection of charity. Holiness is the greatest testimony to the dignity conferred on a disciple of Christ. The Second Vatican Council has significantly spoken on the universal call to holiness. It is possible to say that this call to holiness is precisely the basic charge entrusted to all the sons and daughters of the Church by a Council which intended to bring a renewal of Christian life based on the Gospel.[59]

The call to holiness of life is the universal call for all Church members regardless of their gender or role and official position in their respective church communities. The vocation to holiness encompasses all members of the Church, young and old, men and women. It incorporates those who have been called to the ordained ministry and those who have received the vocation to live their lives as lay members of the Church. All Church members have been called to bear witness to the Gospel of Christ in their daily lives and their respective families, church communities and places of work:

> Everyone in the Church, precisely because they are members, receive and thereby share in the common vocation to holiness. In the fullness of this title and on equal par with all other members of the Church, the lay faithful are called to holiness: 'All the faithful of Christ of whatever rank or status are called to the fullness of Christian life and to the perfection of charity'; 'all of Christ's followers are invited and bound to pursue holiness and the perfect fulfillment of their own state of life.' The call to holiness is rooted in Baptism and proposed anew in the other Sacraments, principally in the Eucharist. Since Christians are re-clothed in Christ Jesus and refreshed by His Spirit, they are

---

ii/en/apost_letters/2001/documents/hf_jp-ii_apl_2001 0106_novo-millennio-ineunte.html (accessed January 19, 2016).

[59] *Christifideles Laici*, 16.

'holy.' They, therefore, have the ability to manifest this holiness and the responsibility to bear witness to it in all that they do.[60]

Members of Christ's Church have also been encouraged to become actively involved in the mission of the Church. As co-workers in the vineyard of the Lord, the lay faithful have been encouraged "to take an active, conscientious and responsible part in the mission of the Church."[61] Since the mission of the Church is directed at the salvation of all mankind, such mission demands an ongoing evangelization and transformation of the temporal order of the world in light of the teachings of the Gospel. Men and women, all members of the Church, share in the three characteristics, the three functions of Christ. Furthermore, they have been commissioned and enabled to go into the world and to evangelize. "There is no doubt that in virtue of Baptism and Confirmation, a woman—as well as a man—is made a sharer in the threefold mission of Jesus Christ, priest, prophet and king, and is thereby charged and given the ability to fulfill the fundamental apostolate of the Church: evangelization."[62] All members of the Church have a unique and personal vocation[63] through which they realize the Lord's call to become co-workers in His vineyard.

All the members of the People of God—clergy, men and women religious, the lay faithful—are laborers in the vineyard. At one and the same time they all are the goal and subjects of Church communion as well as of participation in the mission of salvation. Every one of us possessing charisms and ministries, diverse yet complementary, works in the one and the same vineyard of the Lord.[64]

The process of evangelization is to take place on all levels of the local/particular and universal Church. The lay faithful have been encouraged by John Paul II to a full and active participation in the life of the Church, on both local and universal levels. Saint John Paul II went into great detail in his apostolic exhortation explaining the relationship between a particular (local) Church and the Universal Church. In his teachings, the pope emphasized that while the Universal Church is fully present in each of the particular (local) churches. The Universal Church is not simply the collective tally of all individual (local) churches. By the same token specific (local) church communities are not to be perceived as "local agencies" or "subdivisions" of the Universal Church.

---

[60] *Christifideles Laici,* 16.

[61] Ibid., 3.

[62] Ibid., 51.

[63] *Christifideles Laici,* 28.

[64] Ibid., 55.

For an adequate participation in ecclesial life, the lay faithful absolutely need to have a clear and precise vision of the particular Church with its primordial bond to the universal Church. The particular Church does not come about from a kind of fragmentation of the universal Church nor does the universal Church come about by a simple amalgamation of particular Churches. But there is a real, essential and constant bond uniting each of them, and this is why the universal Church exists and is manifested in the particular Churches. For this reason the Council says that the particular Churches "are constituted after the model of the universal Church; it is in and from these particular Churches that there comes into being the one and unique Catholic Church.[65]

John Paul II reminded various members of the Church that the council fathers considered a parish to be a fundamental cell which thrived in connection with the diocesan church, which in turn fostered the relationship based on unity with the Universal Church.

The same Council strongly encourages the lay faithful actively to live out their belonging to the particular Church, while at the same time assuming an ever-increasing 'catholic' spirit: 'Let the lay faithful constantly foster'—we read in the Decree on the   Apostolate of Lay People - a feeling for their own diocese, of which the parish is a kind of cell, and be always ready at their bishops' invitation to participate in diocesan books…and in the interparochial, inter-diocesan, national and international fields.[66]

Local church communities present around the world in a form of a primary ecclesiastic cell called a parish are "the Church living in the midst of the homes of her sons and daughters."[67] Local parishes are those unique places where baptized members of the Church are being nourished by the Eucharist and send forth for the ministry of service that is inspired by the teachings of the Gospel. A Catholic parish is:

"the place where the very 'mystery' of the Church is present and at work,…The parish is not principally a structure, a territory or a building, but rather 'the family of God, a fellowship afire with a unifying spirit,' 'a familial and welcoming home,' the 'community of the faithful.' Plainly and simply, the parish is founded on a theological reality because it is a Eucharistic community."[68]

---

[65] Ibid., 25.

[66] *Christifideles Laici,* 25.

[67] Ibid.

[68] Ibid., 26.

"Home is where the heart is" and for many Catholics their local parish has been their spiritual home, a community of saints and sinners who have been walking together side by side on their pilgrim journey leading towards salvation and life eternal in God's Kingdom. We sing about this dimension of our faith in one of David Haas' songs called "The Song of the Body of Christ;"

> We come to share our story. We come to break the bread.
> We come to know our rising from the dead.
> We come as your people. We come as your own.
> United with each other, love finds a home.
> We are called to heal the broken, to be hope for the poor.
> We are called to feed the hungry at our door.
> Bread of life and cup of promise, In this meal we all are one.
> In our dying and our rising, may your kingdom come.[69]

Many of God's people are gathered together as one in their local parish churches. They are beckoned to worship and to be re-affirmed in their call to serve others as exampled by Christ. They are summoned to share the Good News of the Gospel with all people God places in their life and faith journey.

At the beginning of his pontificate, Paul VI addressed the Roman clergy in these words: We believe simply that this old and venerable structure of the parish has an indispensable mission of great contemporary importance: to create the basic community of the Christian people; to initiate and gather the people in the accustomed expression of liturgical life; to conserve and renew the faith in the people of today; to serve as the school for teaching the salvific message of Christ; to put solidarity in practice and work the humble charity of good and brotherly works.[70]

Local parish communities have an indisputable role in the process of faith sharing and an ongoing evangelization. In the words of Paul the Apostle; "the charity of Christ impels us,"[71] to go into the world and to preach the Gospel to every creature: "Woe, to me if I do not preach the Gospel."[72] The ongoing need for New Evangelization and Re-Evangelization of Europe and other parts of the world has been expressed by John Paul II in his Apostolic Exhortation: *Ecclesia in Europa,* 2003.

---

[69] David Haas, *The Song of the Body of Christ,* Gather Comprehensive (Chicago: GIA Publications, Inc., 1994), 847.

[70] *Christifideles Laici,* 26. See also Paul VI, Discourse to the Roman Clergy (June 24, 1963): *AAS* 55, 674.

[71] 2 Cor. 5:14.

[72] 1 Cor. 9:16.

Everywhere, then, a renewed proclamation is needed even for those already baptized. Many Europeans today think they know what Christianity is, yet they do not really know it at all. Often they are lacking in knowledge of the most basic elements and notions of the faith. Many of the baptized live as if Christ did not exist: the gestures and signs of faith are repeated, especially in devotional practices, but they fail to correspond to a real acceptance of the content of the faith and fidelity to the person of Jesus. The great certainties of the faith are being undermined in many people by a vague religiosity lacking real commitment; various forms of agnosticism and practical atheism are spreading and serve to widen the division between faith and life.[73]

John Paul II emphasized his concerns regarding the Church in Europe in regard to the spreading secularization, atheism, consumerism and the ever present relativism. The removal of faith from everyday life has been a common practice in the Western European countries of the third millennium as well as in the United States of America. The need for the New Evangelization has never been more pressing in the modern age according to John Paul II. Catholic laity needs to accept their unique and irreplaceable role in the process of spreading the Good News. "The contribution of the lay faithful to the life of the Church is essential: they have an irreplaceable role in the proclamation and the service of the Gospel of hope, since through them the Church of Christ is made present in the various sectors of the world, as a sign and source of hope and of love."[74]

The pontiff was convinced that the European Continent was in a dire need of the new and credible evangelizers: "Europe calls out for credible evangelizers, whose lives, in communion with the Cross and Resurrection of Christ, radiate the beauty of the Gospel."[75] The new evangelizers are those who bear an authentic witness to the Gospel values in their lives by carrying their daily crosses with their eyes fixed on the promise of eternal life and salvation. Theirs is the task to bring the Gospel of hope to all who live in the darkness of sin and despair.

Pope Benedict XVI

The immediate successor of John Paul II, Pope Benedict XVI, on several occasions during his eight years as the Pastor of the Universal Church, addressed the themes of the New Evangelization and the importance of local parish communities in their evangelization efforts. On July 25, 2005, shortly after his election as pope, Benedict XVI met with the diocesan clergy of Aosta, Italy. In his address to priests

---

[73]John Paul II, Post-Synodal Apostolic Exhortation The Church in Europe *Ecclesia in Europa*, (June 28, 2003), 47, Vatican, http://w2.vatican.va/content/john-paul-ii/en/apost_exhortations/documents/hf_jp-ii_exh_20030628_ecclesia-in-europa.html (accessed July 31, 2015). Here after cited as *Ecclesia in Europa*.

[74] *Ecclesia in Europa*, 41.

[75] Ibid., 49.

and pastors, Benedict XVI expressed his concerns regarding the countries of the Western world where the ever present secularism and relativism have rejected the very existence of God and His teachings. When everything becomes subjective, and man has been placed on the pedestal that had been formerly occupied by God, the reversal of moral values follows as a natural consequence. Being a faithful follower of Christ and a committed disciple is not for the faint-hearted in the twenty-first century. Christians and mainly Roman Catholic Christians who commit themselves to the proclamation of Christ's Gospel and the New Evangelization are counter-cultural witnesses to the Risen Lord who lives in our midst. The importance of being a part of a loving and encouraging faith community where one evangelizes and one is being evangelized is without any doubt an essential element of our Christian identity.

Contrary to the convictions of our secularized and individualistic world, we are not lonely sailors on this journey of our life and faith. We are a part of a community of faith which on a local level is called a parish.

Faith essentially creates an assembly and unites. It is precisely this essence of faith that liberates us from egoistic isolation and unites us in a great community, a very complete one - in parishes, in the Sunday gathering, - a universal community in which I become related to everyone in the world. It is necessary to understand this Catholic dimension of the community that gathers in the parish church every Sunday. Thus, if, on the one hand, knowing the faith is one purpose, on the other, socializing in the Church or 'ecclesializing' means being introduced into the great community of the Church, a living milieu, where I know that even in the important moments of my life - especially in suffering and in death - I am not alone.[76]

The primary task of every church community is to actively promote the mission of the Universal Church which is based on two essential aspects: the proclamation of the Good News (*kerygma*[77] – the core teachings of the Gospel based

---

[76] Pope Benedict XVI, *Parish Church at Introd* (July 25, 2005), Aosta Valley, http://w2.vatican.va/ content/benedict-xvi/en/speeches/2005/july/documents/hf_ben-xvi_spe_20050725_diocesi-aosta.html (accessed on July 31, 2015).

[77] Trent C. Butler, ed., *Holman Bible Dictionary* (Nashville, Tennessee: Holman Bible Publishers, 1991), 837-838. The Holman Bible Dictionary provides the following explanation of *kerygma*; Transliteration of the Greek term which means both "the act of preaching" and "the content of the preaching." Preaching in the biblical sense is primarily the act of proclaiming the acts of God. It is more than the ability to speak in beautiful or eloquent words. Preaching in the biblical sense is persuasive because it is done in the Spirit with power (1 Cor. 2:41). God intervenes in the lives of the hearers through the act of preaching; the Kingdom of God comes through the act of preaching (see Matt. 12:41; Luke 11:32). In the act of preaching the hope we have of eternal life is revealed (Titus 1:1-3). The content of preaching in the New Testament centers on Jesus. According to Paul, some see the preaching of a crucified Savior as foolish; but for those who believe it means eternal life (1 Cor. 1:21). Of course, the preaching about Jesus concerns not only His death on a cross but also His resurrection (1 Cor. 15:12). For a more detailed description of *kerygma* refer to James I. H. McDonald, *Kerygma and Didache* (New York: Cambridge University Press, 1980), 1-8.

on the message and the ministry of Jesus) and on giving an authentic witness to the Gospel. The heralding of the Good News is aimed at bringing people to Christ for the sake of their salvation, accepting his teachings and changing their lives in light of the Gospel, which ultimately leads to conversion.

Pope Benedict XVI reiterated his convictions and beliefs regarding the need for Christian witness and the proclamation of the Gospel on May 27, 2007, in his "Letter to the Bishops, Priests, Consecrated Persons and Lay Faithful of the Catholic Church in the People's Republic of China."[78] In his letter the Universal Pastor of the Church emphasized the importance of the missionary nature of the Church and the proclamation of the Gospel of Jesus Christ based on everyday witness;

> Today, as in the past, to proclaim the Gospel means to preach and bear witness to Jesus Christ, crucified and risen, the new Man, conqueror of sin and death. He enables human beings to enter into a new dimension, where mercy and love shown even to enemies can bear witness to the victory of the Cross over all weakness and human wretchedness.[79]…The Church, always and everywhere missionary, is called to proclaim and to bear witness to the Gospel. The Church in China must also sense in her heart the missionary ardor of her Founder and Teacher.[80]

Three years later Benedict XVI re-visited the subjects of evangelization and the universal call for the Church and all of her members to proclaim the Gospel. Inspired by his zeal for the Church that is called to evangelize and to be evangelized at the same time, Benedict XVI established in June of 2010 the Pontifical Council for the Promotion of the New Evangelization. He also made a decision to convene the XIII Ordinary General Assembly of the Synod of Bishops from October 7 through October 28, 2012. The main topic of the synod was: *The New Evangelization for the Transmission of the Christian Faith.* In preparation for the synod, Benedict XVI also proclaimed and inaugurated on October 11, 2011, the Year of Faith[81] that was to begin on October 11, 2012, the fiftieth anniversary of the opening of the Second Vatican Council. Benedict XVI believed very strongly in supporting various efforts for the promotion of the New Evangelization. In his eyes, the proclamation of the

---

[78]Benedict XVI, *Letter to the Bishops, Priests, Consecrated Persons and Lay Faithful of the Catholic Church in the People's Republic of China,* (May 27, 2007), Vatican, http://w2.vatican.va/content/benedict-xvi/en/letters/2007/documents/hf_ben-xvi_let_20070527_china.html (accessed August 1, 2015).

[79] Ibid., 3.

[80] Ibid., 17.

[81] Benedict XVI, Apostolic Letter "Motu Proprio Data," For The Indiction of The Year of Faith *Porta Fidei,* (October 11, 2011), Vatican, http://w2.vatican.va/content/benedict-xvi/en/motu_proprio/ documents/hf_ben-xvi_motu-proprio_20111011_porta-fidei.html (accessed January 19, 2016). Here after cited as *Porta Fidei.*

kerygma should lead people to a personal encounter and a personal relationship with Jesus Christ.

This new way of looking at evangelization kept reappearing in the pope's teachings on several different occasions. In his address to the Philipino bishops during their *ad Limina Apostolorum* visit in the Vatican City State on May 3, 2011, Benedict XVI stated:

> Your great task in evangelization is, therefore, to propose a personal relationship with Christ as key to complete fulfilment...At the same time, it must be recognized that new initiatives in evangelization will only be fruitful if, by the grace of God, those proposing them are people who truly believe and live the message of the Gospel themselves. This is surely one of the reasons why basic ecclesial communities have had such a positive impact throughout the country. When formed and guided by people whose motivating force is the love of Christ, these communities have proven themselves to be worthy tools of evangelization as they work in conjunction with local parishes.[82]

Evangelization efforts should lead to the conversion of those being evangelized in order to develop a strong and personal relationship with Jesus Christ. Present day evangelists ought to proclaim the Good News by word and by example. The faith that they profess with their lips is a living faith that requires an authentic witness to the Gospel of Christ in their daily lives. Nothing in this world is capable of providing the ultimate happiness and satisfaction for modern people and especially for the youth of our times. The New Evangelization needs to assist young women and men to reawaken in their hearts and minds a longing for a personal relationship with God and with other members of a Christian community.

> In order to confront the questions of our times, the laity need to hear the Gospel message in its fullness, to understand its implications for their personal lives and for society in general, and thus be constantly converted to the Lord. I, therefore, urge you to take special care in shepherding such groups, so that the primacy of God may remain in the forefront. This primacy is of particular importance when it comes to the evangelization of youth. I encourage you to continue to remind young people that the glamour of this world will not satisfy their natural desire for happiness. Only true friendship with God will break the bonds of loneliness from which our fragile humanity suffers and will establish a true and lasting communion with others, a spiritual bond that will

---

[82] Benedict XVI, *Address to the Bishops of the Episcopal Conference of the Philippines on Their Ad Limina Visit,* (February 18, 2011), Vatican, https://w2.vatican.va/content/benedict-xvi/en/speeches/2011/ february/documents /hf_ben-xvi_spe_20110218_bishops-philippines.html (accessed January 19, 2016).

readily prompt within us the wish to serve the needs of those we love in Christ.[83]

Benedict XVI emphasized the need for a personal encounter with Jesus which ultimately should lead to the development of a personal relationship with Him. Although this concept is hardly a new development in the theology of the Church, it has been mostly overtly associated with the Protestant Churches. Many Roman Catholics become suspicious when they hear about "having a personal relationship with their Savior." However, many members of the Church forget that throughout the history of salvation we have witnessed vast numbers of ordinary people, prophets, and kings, saints and sinners who experienced a personal encounter with the living God. This unique encounter had changed their lives and had motivated them throughout the course of their earthly journeys to foster their close and personal relationship with God. The Bible is replete with many such examples as are more recent times: Abraham, Moses, Solomon, David, Blessed Virgin Mary, St. Paul, St. Peter, St. Matthew, St. Francis, Mother Theresa, St. John Paul II, Thomas Merton, mystics such as St. Therese of Lisieux, Padre Pio, St. Faustina Kowalska and many others. In the Catholic tradition, the encounter with the living God is an encounter with the Holy Trinity. When we encounter the person of Jesus and learn about Him and His teachings, we are being led by the Holy Spirit into a deeper and fuller relationship with the living God who reveals Himself in the ordinary moments of our lives. In this sense, the New Evangelization can be understood as a personal encounter and relationship with the Triune God. This concept of a personal encounter with Christ leading to a personal relationship with Him has been one of the focal points of the document released prior to the XIII Ordinary General Assembly of the Synod of Bishops convened in October, 2012. The *Lineamenta,* "the guidelines," described the most pressing issues and challenges facing the Church in the post-modern world. These challenges refer to six different areas of the present day human society: culture, society, social communication, scientific and technological research, the economy, civic and political life. The *Lineamenta* underlined the need for the New Evangelization understood as a new way of proclaiming the Gospel of Christ (the context remains the same) to all believers in order to deepen their faith and relationship with Christ. The efforts of the New Evangelization are also aimed at the proclamation of the Good News of the Gospel to the non-practicing baptized members of the Church who for whatever reason have drifted away from their faith and religious practices. New Evangelization is aimed at developing new ways and means for the proclamation of the Gospel and the transmission of the faith.

Evangelization is at the very heart of the Church's fundamental mission. All members of the Church have been entrusted with the mission to proclaim the Gospel and to bear an authentic witness to its teachings in their daily lives.

---

[83] Benedict XVI, *Address to the Bishops of the Episcopal Conference of the Philippines on Their Ad Limina Visit,* (February 18, 2011), Vatican, https://w2.vatican.va/content/benedict-xvi/en/speeches/2011/ february/ documents / hf_ben-xvi_spe_20110218_bishops-philippines.html (accessed January 19, 2016).

Presently, in reviewing the dynamics of the 'new evangelization,' the expression can now be applied to the Church's renewed efforts to meet the challenges which today's society and cultures, in view of the significant changes taking place, are posing to the Christian faith, its proclamation and its witness. In facing these challenges, the Church does not give up or retreat into herself; instead, she undertakes a book to revitalize herself. She makes the Person of Jesus Christ and a personal encounter with him central to her thinking, knowing that he will give his Spirit and provide the force to announce and proclaim the Gospel in new ways which can speak to today's cultures.[84]

The missionary mandate expressed in the Gospels (Mk. 16:15-17, Mt. 28:19-20, Lk. 24:48-49) continues to be as valid today as it was during the earthly ministry of Jesus. The Church exists to go into the world and to proclaim the Gospel of Christ. Her missionary and evangelizing efforts are meant to be *ad intra* and *ad extra.* The Church is both the proclaimer and the hearer. She is evangelizing and she is being evangelized at the same time. In the words of *Lineamenta:*

> missionary activity *ad intra* is a credible sign and a stimulus for missionary activity *ad extra*, and vice versa. Being Christian and 'being Church' means being missionary; one is or is not. Loving one's faith implies bearing witness to it, bringing it to others and allowing others to participate in it. The lack of missionary zeal is a lack of zeal for the faith. On the contrary, faith is made stronger by transmitting it.[85]

The goal of proclaiming the Gospel and spreading the faith presupposes a personal encounter with Jesus, which leads to a deeper relationship with the Holy Trinity. "Consequently, the goal of the transmission of the faith is the realization of a personal encounter with Jesus Christ, in the Spirit, thereby leading to an experiencing of his Father and our Father."[86] Following Christ and embracing the teachings of the Gospel in our daily lives (our families, workplaces and communities) is a disciple's response to a personal encounter with Jesus Christ. It is a loving response of a faithful disciple who experienced God's unconditional love and who now wishes to extend that love to others. In the words of Pope Benedict XVI: "We have come to believe in God's love: in these words the Christian can express the fundamental decision of his life. Being Christian is not the result of an ethical choice or a lofty idea, but the

---

[84] Synod of Bishops, The XIII Ordinary General Assembly: *The New Evangelization for the Transmission of the Christian Faith, Lineamenta*, (February 11, 2011), 5, Vatican, http://www.vatican. va/roman_curia/synod/ documents/rc_synod_doc_20120619_instrumentum-xiii_en.pdf (accessed August 5, 2015). Here after cited as *Lineamenta.*

[85] *Lineamenta*, 10.

[86] *Lineamenta*, 11.

encounter with an event, a person, which gives life a new horizon and a decisive direction."[87]

In other words, a personal encounter with the person and the event of Jesus Christ

> "allows individuals to share in the Son's relationship with his Father and to experience the power of the Spirit. The aim of transmitting the faith and the goal of evangelization is to bring us 'through him [Christ] in one Spirit to the Father' (Eph 2:18)."[88] Every Christian and the entire Church have been entrusted with the task of proclaiming the Gospel and transmitting the faith. In doing so, the followers of Jesus Christ are called to demonstrate the essential elements of the life of faith such as "charity, witness, proclamation, celebration, and sharing."[89] Furthermore, the example of a real life of faith has been clearly manifested by the early Christian communities which should become an inspiration for the modern day local church communities entrusted with the task of evangelization and the transmission of the faith:

> > The agent for transmitting the faith is the entire Church which manifests itself in the local Churches, where proclamation, transmission and the lived experience of the Gospel are realized. Furthermore, the local Churches, in addition to performing this task, are also   the fruit of this activity of proclaiming the Gospel and transmitting the faith, as seen in the experience of the first Christian communities (Acts 2: 42-47). The Spirit gathers believers into communities that fervently live their faith, a faith which is nourished through listening to the teaching of the apostles, through the Eucharist and through the communities' life of unselfish service to proclaiming the Kingdom of God.[90]

The local church that many of the faithful refer to as their local parish or their home church has an indispensable role in the process of the new evangelization and the transmission of the faith. Understood as a "community of communities," the local parish church is an entryway for many people who wish to encounter Jesus Christ and become his missionary disciples. As a living and breathing organism, the local parish is capable of becoming a fertile ground for the transmission of the faith, for the formation of intentional disciples, and for authentic witness to the Gospel of Jesus

---

[87] Benedict XVI, Encyclical Letter: God is Love *Deus Caritas Est,* (December 25, 2005), 1, Vatican,.http://w2.vatican.va/content/benedict-xvi/en/encyclicals/documents/hf_ben-xvi_enc_20051225_deus-caritas-est.html (accessed January 19, 2016). Here after cited as *Deus Caritas Est.*

[88] *Lineamenta,* 11.

[89] Ibid.

[90] Ibid., 15.

Christ. Through its missionary and evangelizing efforts *ad intra* and *ad extra,* local parish communities have the ability to form intentional disciples of Christ who are committed to bring Christ to others, their families, workplaces and communities where they live and come in contact with other people. Parishes ought to be more concerned about their evangelization efforts and the outreach to the larger community where they exist and function rather than their self-preservation. Parish church communities are those sacred communities where the love of Christ for all people must be proclaimed and exemplified through a day-to-day witness to the faith professed with the lips of the diverse parish members. *The Instrumentum Laboris* for the New Evangelization for the Transmission of the Christian Faith states:

> The new evangelization is a call to the Church to rediscover her missionary origins. According to many responses, the new evangelization can devote work in this area to leading Christian communities to be less concentrated on themselves inwardly in the midst of the changes already taking place and more engaged in proclaiming the faith to others. In this regard, much is expected from parishes that are seen as an entryway, open to everyone in every place on the globe, to the Christian faith and an experience of the Church.[91]

The role of a local parish community in the process of the new evangelization and the transmission of the faith is paramount. Local parish churches ought to become an oasis of Christian life and witness to the Gospel of Christ:

> …parishes have the responsibility to become real centers for propagating and bearing witness to the Christian experience and places for attentively listening to people and ascertaining their needs. Parishes are places where a person receives instruction on searching for the truth, where faith is nourished and strengthened and where the Christian message and God's plan for humanity and the world is communicated. They are the   prime communities for experiencing the joy that comes from being not only gathered together by the Spirit but prepared to live one's proper vocation as a missionary.[92]

The role of a local parish in the process of evangelizing and making intentional disciples can never be underestimated. For many Roman Catholics, their local parish is the first and sacred place where they have learned about God and where they have deepened their faith through catechesis and Christian service. It is their home away from home where saints and sinners come together with their

---

[91] Synod of Bishops, The XIII Ordinary General Assembly: *The New Evangelization for the Transmission of the Christian Faith,* Instrumentum Laboris, (June 19, 2012), 81, Vatican, http://www.vatican.va/roman_curia/synod/documents/rc_synod_doc_20120619_instrumentum-xiii_en.html#The _Question_of_a_New_Evangelization (accessed January 19, 2016). Here after cited as *Instrumentum Laboris.*

[92] *Instrumentum Laboris,* 81.

brokenness, trials, and tribulations. In their local parish, they find solace as they gather together at the Eucharistic table and as they listen to the Word of God. They are being gathered by "the love of Christ which fills their hearts and impels them to evangelize."[93]

Pope Francis

After the surprising resignation of Pope Benedict XVI on February 28, 2013, the Catholic faithful and many people around the world were in a state of complete shock. Concerned about the well-being of the entire Church and his own ability to exercise effectively the Petrine Office, Pope Benedict XVI decided to step down and make room for a new leader of the Catholic Church. Cardinal Jorge Mario Bergogliowas elected by a majority vote on March 13, 2013, the second day of the conclave. The former Archbishop of the Diocese of Buenos Aires in Argentina, chose the name Francis, and became the Pastor of the Universal Church. By accepting the electoral vote, Pope Francis became the leader of 1.2 billion Catholics around the world.

From the early days of his papacy, Pope Francis began to reform the Catholic Church starting with the Roman Curia through the scrutiny of the questionable financial practices at the Vatican Bank. To date, there has been hardly any aspect of the Church's life and ministry that Pope Francis has not addressed or talked about in his teachings. Without any doubt, the seventy-nine years old pontiff has set a new course for the Catholic Church based on openness, transparency, dialog and collaboration.

From the early days of his pontificate, Pope Francis called upon all Catholics - lay and ordained-members-to transform the face of the Catholic Church in the Third Millennium by making it more welcoming and more open to the people living in the post-modern culture. Considered by many as "the people's pope," Francis, through his unpretentious words and actions, continues to draw people closer to God and His Church. In his teachings, Pope Francis calls upon all members of the Church to re-discover their call to discipleship and to become actively involved in the missionary activity of the Church. He has encouraged all members of the Church "to go out into the streets," and to bear witness to the Gospel of Christ and His teachings. In his address to the young people from Argentina who gathered in Rio de Janeiro in Brazil for the International World Youth Day, Pope Francis stated: "I want the Church to go out onto the streets. I want us to resist everything worldly, everything static, everything comfortable, everything to do with clericalism, everything that might make us closed in on ourselves. The parishes, the schools, the institutions are made for going out."[94]

---

[93] *Porta Fidei*, 7.
[94] Pope Francis, Address During a Meeting With the Young People from Argentina, Apostolic Journey to Rio De Janeiro on the Occasion of the XXVIII World Youth Day, (July 25, 2013), Rio De

Pope Francis calls upon all Church members to become missionary disciples who by their word and example proclaim the Gospel and bring people closer to God. In his teachings, Pope Francis has underlined the communal dimension of the Catholic faith in contrast with the ever-present individualism and selfishness exhibited in the modern day society.

> The Church is born from God's wish to call all people to communion with him, to friendship with him, indeed, to share in his own divine life as his sons and daughters. The very word 'Church,' from the Greek *ekklesia*, means 'convocation': God convokes us, he impels us to come out of our individualism, from our tendency to close ourselves into ourselves, and he calls us to belong to his family.[95]

In his eyes, the Church must re-discover her missionary identity lest she becomes a stagnant Church preoccupied with her self-preservation. Members of the Church create a unique family through which they enter into a communion with God and with one another. God calls all members of Christ's Church to be a part of the human family and to engage in the ministry of service on behalf of Christ and His Church. In a very special way as missionary disciples, members of the Church have been called to reach out to those who are poor and hungry and those who live on the margins of our society; the outcasts and the marginalized. By going out into the world, the followers of Jesus Christ will be able to encounter a variety of people and experience their living conditions first hand. In doing so, the missionary disciples will be able to transform the world in the light and the spirit of the Gospel. Despite the sinfulness and imperfections of church members, God continues to reach out to His people by offering them His love and mercy. "Through her visible reality, all that can be seen, the sacraments and witness of all us Christians, the Church is called every day to be close to every man, to begin with the one who is poor, the one who suffers and the one who is marginalized, in such a way as to make all people feel the compassionate and merciful gaze of Jesus."[96]

On several different occasions, Pope Francis has spoken about the importance of a local church community and the ongoing need to renew its apostolic enthusiasm in the process of evangelization. The pope has emphasized the need for parish members to make themselves available to other people and to be creative while getting engaged in the ministry of service. In his address to Catholic Action Italy, the

---

Janeiro, https://w2.vatican.va/content/francesco/en/speeches/2013/july/documents/papa-francesco_20130725_ gmg-argentini-rio.html (accessed January 19, 2016).

[95] Pope Francis, General Audience, (May 29, 2013), Vatican, https://w2.vatican.va/content/ francesco/en/audiences/2013/documents/papa francesco_20130529_udienza-generale.html (accessed August 9, 2015).

[96] Pope Francis, Weekly General Audience, (October 29, 2014), Vatican, https://w2.vatican.va/ content/francesco/en/audiences/2014/documents/papa-francesco_20141029_udienza-generale.html (accessed August 10, 2015).

largest lay Catholic organization in Italy, Pope Francis stated: "In the first place, parishes, especially those marked by fatigue and closures - and there are many of them - need your apostolic enthusiasm, your availability and your full creative service…. In the current social and ecclesial context, you lay people of Catholic Action are called to renew your missionary commitment."[97]

The Pope encourages lay people to become living examples and witnesses to the Gospel of Christ in their communities, families and workplaces. During his two-and-a- half year long pontificate, Pope Francis has given significant attention to local parishes and basic ecclesial communities as doorways leading to a personal encounter with Christ and His message. Catholic parishes have an essential role in the process of engaging their diverse members in the universal mission of the entire *Body of Christ:* to proclaim the Good News by words and actions. Parish communities should become communities built on love, compassion, and unity. Members of local church communities need to careful not to fall into "parish sins," expressed by a tendency of some members to be judgmental of others, critical, envious and above all divisive.

> The Apostle Paul then exhorted his communities not to forget that they are 'one body' (1 Corinthians 12:13). However, experience tells us that there are many sins against unity. And we do not think only of the great heresies and the schisms; we think of the many common failures in our communities, of 'parish' sins, at those sins in the parishes. Sometimes, in fact, our parishes, called to be places of sharing and communion, are marked sadly by envies, jealousies, antipathies. And this chitchat is carried to all. How much this chitchat exists in the parishes! This is not good. […] This is not the Church! One must not do this; we must not do it! We need to ask the Lord for the grace not to do this. This is human, all right, but not Christian! This happens when we seek the first places, when we put ourselves at the center, with our personal ambitions and our ways of seeing things, and we judge others; when we look at the defects of our brothers instead of their gifts, when we give more weight to what divides that to what brings us together.[98]

Committed disciples of Jesus Christ are called to imitate Christ and to live by His teachings day in and day out. Pope Francis encourages church communities to go out into the world and to give witness to Jesus' teachings and to transform the world by living in accordance with the values of the Gospels. Catholic Church communities (parishes) are not formed for the purpose of becoming exclusive "clubs." Parish communities have been created not just for the privileged few who are more concerned about self-preservation and self-service than the evangelizing mission of the Universal Church. Parish church communities should become places of love,

---

[97] Pope Francis, Address to the Members of the Catholic Action Italy, (May 5, 2014), Vatican, http://www.zenit.org/en/articles/pope-to-lay-people-parishes-need-you (accessed August 10, 2015).

[98] Pope Francis, General Audience (August 27, 2014), Vatican, http://www.zenit.org/en/articles /on-the-dangers-of-parish-sins (accessed August 10, 2015).

compassion, and unbiased acceptance where rich and poor are welcomed at the table of plenty. Pope Francis expressed this part of his teachings in his 2015 Lenten message:

> Every Christian community is called to go out of itself and to be engaged in the life of the greater society of which it is a part, especially with the poor and those who are far away. The Church is missionary by her very nature; she is not self-enclosed but sent out to every nation and people. Her mission is to bear patient witness to the One who desires to draw all creation and every man and woman to the Father. Her mission is to bring to all a love which cannot remain silent. The Church follows Jesus Christ along the paths that lead to every man and woman, to the very ends of the earth (cf. Acts 1:8). In each of our neighbors, then, we must see a brother or sister for whom Christ died and rose again.   What we ourselves have received, we have received for them as well. Similarly, all that our brothers and sisters possess is a gift for the Church and for all humanity.[99]

Solidarity with the rest of humanity and an open dialog with those who come in contact with Christians are the integral parts of the process of evangelization. The gift of the Church just like many other gifts bestowed on church communities and particular individuals should be shared with all people for the greater benefit of the entire human family. A local parish church community needs to become a family of families[100] where all people feel welcome in the spirit of Christian love and charity. Members of parish communities are called to be there for one another during times of joy and sorrow. Furthermore, each and every member of a parish community has been called to participate in the mission of the Universal Church. They are called to proclaim by words and actions God's love for all people, so that all can be saved.

On November 24, 2013, Pope Francis released his Apostolic Exhortation *Evangelii Gaudium* (The Joy of the Gospel). This important document authored by Pope Francis was released at the end of The Year of Faith promulgated by his predecessor Pope Benedict XVI. *Evangelii Gaudium* presents several essential subjects regarding the new evangelization and the life of the Church which had been discussed during the XIII Ordinary Synod of Bishops in 2012 at the Vatican City State under the title: *The New Evangelization for the Transmission of the Christian Faith.* In his apostolic exhortation Pope Francis reminded all Christian faithful about the necessity of a personal relationship with Jesus Christ and His Body, the Church, which can nurture our faith and help us to become joyful evangelizers in our post-modern world. Pope Francis called upon all Church members to become missionary

---

[99] Pope Francis, Lenten Message 2015: *Make Your Hearts Firm,* (October 4, 2014), Vatican, https://w2.vatican.va/content/francesco/en/messages/lent/documents/papa-francesco_20141004_messaggio-quaresima2015.html (accessed August 10, 2015).

[100] Benedict XVI, Homily for the Mass and Dedication of the New Parish of St. Corbinian at Infernetto, (March 20, 2011), Rome, http://w2.vatican.va/content/benedict xvi/en/homilies/2011/documents/hf_ben-xvi_hom_20110320_san-corbiniano.html (accessed August 14, 2015).

disciples – people who are willing to go outside of their comfort zones to bring Jesus' Gospel to others. All followers of Jesus Christ have been entrusted with the mission to proclaim the Gospel of Christ in the context of a particular culture that is a part of the daily lives of God's people. According to Pope Francis, the current economic model based on consumer capitalism leads the present day people to individualism characterized by indifference towards others. The distribution of goods is based on inequality where the mighty and the powerful can have it all while the poor and the marginalized are being forced to live on the scraps that fall from their masters' tables. Pope Francis is convinced that the prevailing socioeconomic system is unjust, and it needs to be changed in light of the teachings of the Gospel:

> When a society – whether local, national or global – is willing to leave a part of itself on the fringes, no political programs or resources spent on law enforcement or surveillance systems can indefinitely guarantee tranquility. This is not the case simply because inequality provokes a violent reaction from those excluded from the system, but because the socioeconomic system is unjust at its root.[101]

The Church's evangelization efforts should lead those who listen to the proclamation of the Gospel to a personal encounter with Jesus Christ. This personal encounter ought to direct the people towards a conversion of their hearts and minds in such a way that they will be open and willing to become missionary disciples and spirit-filled evangelizers.[102] In her missionary efforts aimed at the New Evangelization (Pope Francis called it "a new chapter of Evangelization"), the Church must not forget about the fundamental part of her missionary activity, namely, the preferential love/option for the poor. The Church and all of her members must not walk indifferently by the weakest and often forgotten people in our society: the poor and the homeless, the addicted, the refugees, indigenous people, the elderly, the migrants, the victims of human trafficking and the unborn.[103]

The so called first world countries cannot turn their backs away from the most vulnerable members of the society and especially from the migrants who often risk their lives in search of peace and shelter. While running away from their homelands, stricken by violence and war, many migrants die in the process because of the lack of proper means to cross the seas and the desserts or at the hands of human smugglers. Families have been torn apart, and human lives have been lost because the international community does not have a definite plan of action how to address this

---

[101] Pope Francis, Apostolic Exhortation The Joy of the Gospel *Evangelii Gaudium,* (November 24, 2013), 59, Vatican, http://w2.vatican.va/content/francesco/en/apost_exhortations/documents/papa-francesco_esortazione-ap_20131124_evangelii-gaudium.html (accessed August 16, 2015). Here after cited as *Evangelii Gaudium.*

[102] *Evangelii Gaudium*, no. 259-288.

[103] Ibid., 210.

problem. As a matter of fact in the last fifteen years, 22,000 migrants have died while trying to cross over to Europe. The total number of all migrants who have lost their lives all over the world (including the European migrants) during the same period of time is estimated to be at least at 40,000.[104] Although this number is significantly underestimated, the problems of human migration and human trafficking have been on the constant rise in the last two decades. Pope Francis made it very clear in *Evangelii Gaudium* and in his other writings[105] that all people of the world have a moral responsibility to help those most in need: the migrants, the refugees and the poor among us. The Pope believes that since God has a special place in His heart for the poor and the underprivileged, so must the followers of Christ embrace that kind of love in their outreach to the poor of this world. In his own words:

> For the Church, the option for the poor is primarily a theological category rather than a   cultural, sociological, political or philosophical one. God shows the poor 'his first mercy.' This divine preference has consequences for the faith life of all Christians, since we are called to have this mind… which was in Jesus Christ (Phil 2:5). Inspired by this, the Church has made an option for the poor which is understood as a 'special form of primacy in the exercise of Christian charity, to which the whole tradition of the Church bears witness.'…This is why I want a Church, which is poor and for the poor.[106]

Every particular Christian and all Church communities are called to listen to the poor, to respond to their needs and concerns, and to recognize the dignity of every human person. The poor themselves with their *sensus fidei,* their love for God; and because of their immersion in the sufferings of Christ, they are capable of becoming the new evangelizers. All Christians and especially Church members are called to put their faith into action by reaching out and speaking on behalf of the poor, the underprivileged and the marginalized.

Local Catholic parishes have a very unique role in the process of The New Evangelization. Parishes should become family centers where new evangelizers are being formed and where they discover their identity as missionary disciples.

---

[104] International Organization for Migration; *Fatal Journeys, Tracking Lives Lost During Migration,* (2014), Geneva, Switzerland, http://publications.iom.int/bookstore/free/FatalJourneys_Countingthe Uncounted.pdf (accessed August 17, 2015).

[105] Pope Francis, 2015 Message for the 101st World Day of Migrants and Refugees, (September 3, 2014), Vatican, https://w2.vatican.va/content/francesco/en/messages/migration/documents/papa-francesco_20140903_ world-migrants-day-2015.html and *Solidarity for Lampedusa Migrants,* (2013), Vatican, http://en.radiovaticana.va/storico/2013?10/07/pope_francis_solidarity_for_lampedusa_ migrants/en1-735133. (accessed August 17, 2015).

[106] *Evangelii Gaudium,* 197-199.

The parish is not an outdated institution; precisely because it possesses great flexibility, it can assume quite different contours depending on the openness and missionary creativity of the pastor and the community. While certainly not the only institution which evangelizes, if the parish proves capable of self-renewal and constant adaptivity, it continues to be 'the Church living in the midst of the homes of her sons and daughters.' This presumes that it really is in contact with the homes and the lives of its people, and does not become a useless structure out of touch with people or a self-absorbed group made up of a chosen few. The parish is the presence of the Church in a given territory, an environment for hearing God's word, for growth in the Christian life, for dialog, proclamation, charitable outreach, worship and celebration. In all its activities, the parish encourages and trains its members to be evangelizers. It is a community of communities, a sanctuary where the thirsty come to drink in the midst of their journey, and a center of constant missionary outreach. We must admit, though, that the call to review and renew our parishes has not yet sufficed to bring them nearer to people, to make them environments of living communion and participation, and to make them completely mission-oriented.[107]

There is no doubt in the pope's mind that Catholic parishes, in order to become effective centers of the New Evangelization, need to be evangelized themselves. Catholic parishes and their members need to be open to a constant renewal and a conversion process leading them to become the mission-oriented centers of the New Evangelization. Through the development of a parish vision, pastoral planning and conscientious efforts aimed at the formation of missionary disciples, local parishes are capable of transforming themselves into evangelizing communities. Members of such mission-oriented church communities will become active evangelizers proficient enough to change the world in light of Christ's teachings and those of the Gospel's. The Church local and universal must not be afraid to engage the modern day cultures to proclaim the Good News to all people. This reality is especially true for those who live in large urban centers where they are being exposed to a melting pot of diverse cultures and religious beliefs. Furthermore, people living in large cities are being exposed not only to different beliefs and cultures; they are also experiencing first-hand different ideologies and value systems that very often stand in direct opposition to the message of the Gospel. There is a great need in all Catholic parishes and Christian communities to open the doors to their churches and the doors of their hearts to all of God's children without any bias or prejudice. As disciples of the Lord Jesus we have been called to seek the lost, to reach out to those who have left the Catholic Church (for whatever reason) and to minister to those who continue their search for God. The Church must be at the service of all of God's children. She must be more dedicated to the mission of the New Evangelization rather than to the temptations of self-preservation and self-service. At the very beginning of *Evangelii Gaudium,* Pope Francis stated:

---

[107] Ibid., 28.

I dream of a 'missionary option,' that is, a missionary impulse capable of transforming everything, so that the Church's customs, ways of doing things, times and schedules, language and structures can be suitably channeled for the evangelization of today's world rather than for her self-preservation. The renewal of structures demanded by pastoral conversion can only be understood in this light: as part of an effort to make them more   mission-oriented, to make ordinary pastoral activity on every level more inclusive and open, to inspire in pastoral workers a constant desire to go forth and in this way to elicit a positive response from all those whom Jesus summons to friendship with himself.[108]

Pope Francis has called upon the Church and all of her members to rise above the "self-preservation mode" and to embrace the missionary call which is the very reason for the Church's existence. The Church and all Christians are being called upon by Pope Francis to become actively engaged in the evangelization efforts and to transform the world in light of the Gospels. Evangelizing Christian communities need to present the message of the Gospel (*kerygma*), by always searching for new ways and means of expressions. All members of the Church are called to evangelize and to become missionary disciples. Committed evangelizers must not be afraid to seek the lost, to welcome the outcasts and to speak on behalf of the poor and the marginalized.

In virtue of their baptism, all the members of the People of God have become missionary disciples (Mt 28:19). All the baptized, whatever their position in the Church or their level of instruction in the faith, are agents of evangelization, and it would be insufficient to envisage a plan of evangelization to be carried out by professionals while the rest of the faithful would simply be passive recipients. The new evangelization calls for personal involvement on the part of each of the baptized. Every Christian is challenged, here and now, to be actively engaged in evangelization; indeed, anyone who has truly experienced God's saving love does not need much time or lengthy training to go out and proclaim that love. Every Christian is a missionary to the extent that he or she has encountered the love of God in Christ Jesus: we no longer say that we are 'disciples' and 'missionaries,' but rather that we are always missionary disciples.[109]

Local parishes have an indispensable role in the process of the New Evangelization and formation of the missionary disciples. Every local parish community ought to become a "family of families" and "a community of communities" where people can encounter the presence of the living God in the celebration of the sacraments and their interactions with one another. Local parish communities are called by Pope Francis to become centers of faith and evangelization where people come to get to know and to love Jesus, and where Jesus helps them to

---

[108] *Evangelii Gaudium*, 27.

[109] Ibid., 120.

become committed missionary disciples who have been set on fire by the Holy Spirit continuing to guide the Church toward salvation. "In fidelity to the example of the Master, it is of vital importance for the Church today to go forth and preach the Gospel to all: to all places, on all occasions, without hesitation, reluctance or fear. The joy of the Gospel is for all people: no one can be excluded."[110]

Pope Francis underlined the problems and challenges that face present day evangelizers. The influence of secularism and relativism in the post-modern culture cannot be underestimated. Also, Pope Francis has emphasized the need for a reform of the Church so that she may re-discover her missionary spirit and be at the service of humanity. The Church must not remain stagnant – she has to keep moving forward. Christians are called to engage the world and to bring the message of the Good News of Jesus Christ to all people. The pontiff reminded all followers of Christ that the Gospel cannot be limited to "me and my God" experience nor should it be downgraded to a total sum of good deeds one performs in the name of Christ. All members of the Church are encouraged to reflect their love for God in the love of thy neighbors.

> Loving others is a spiritual force drawing us to union with God; indeed, one who does not love others 'walks in the darkness' (1 Jn 2:11), 'remains in death' (1 Jn 3:14) and 'does not know God' (1 Jn 4:8). Benedict XVI has said that 'closing our eyes to our neighbor also blinds us to God,' and that love is, in the end, the only light which 'can always illuminate a world grown dim and give us the courage needed to keep living and working.' When we live out a spirituality of drawing nearer to others and seeking their welfare, our hearts are opened wide to the Lord's greatest and most beautiful gifts. Whenever we encounter another person in love, we learn something new about God. Whenever our eyes are opened to acknowledge the other, we grow in the light of faith and knowledge of God. If we want to advance in the spiritual life, then, we must constantly be missionaries. The work of evangelization enriches the mind and the heart; it opens up spiritual horizons; it makes us more and more sensitive to the workings of the Holy Spirit, and it takes us beyond our limited spiritual constructs.[111]

The Gospel of Christ should compel all members of the Church to participate actively in the building of the Kingdom of God in our midst. This active engagement of the followers of Christ in the process of building God's Kingdom can challenge and transform the systems of social injustice. Furthermore, members of Christ's Church have been called to live their lives in solidarity with the poor and the outcast of our society. Pope Francis has called upon all members of the Church to become "a listening Church." He characterized a listening Church as a Church that is open to listening and to hearing the voices of all of her children (lay and ordained) and the concerns of all of her members. A listening Church should be open to the many

---

[110] *Evangelii Gaudium*, 23.

[111] *Evangelii Gaudium*, 272.

voices of her diverse members. A listening Church ought to be inclusive rather than exclusive.

She is called to respond to the needs of all of her members and not just the privileged few. Guided by the Spirit of the Living God, Church members must do everything in their power to end inequality and the exploitation of the poor. The New Evangelization needs to be based on a collaborative dialog between the Church and the post-modern world. Such dialog is to take place on the political, social, religious and cultural levels of the human society. The Church is in desperate need of "spirit filled" evangelizers who through their personal encounter with Jesus Christ become open to the guidance of the Holy Spirit forming them as bold, missionary disciples. The Church must be keenly aware at all times that she exists in order to proclaim the Gospel of Christ and to bear witness to her founder. Every Catholic parish becomes a privileged place of listening where the Gospel of Christ is being proclaimed and where the new evangelizers are being formed in the spirit of missionary disciples: "Every parish is called to be a privileged place of listening and of the proclamation of the Gospel; a house of prayer gathered around the Eucharist; a true school of communion, where the ardour of charity prevails over the temptation of a superficial and dry religiosity."[112]

For such parishes to be established and to be able to form others as active agents of the New Evangelization Catholic parishes must renew and rediscover their missionary identity and become centers of welcoming and faith-nurturing communities.

The Catholic Parish: Criteria for Vitality and Mission

Criteria for Parish Vitality

In an effort to develop various pastoral plans for Catholic parishes in transition, numerous dioceses in the United States have issued detailed lists and plans containing the criteria for parish vitality. Although these criteria may differ from one diocese to another, (for example, in the number of listed characteristics and emphasis on specific attributes found in vital parishes), there have been several common factors listed as key characteristics of vital parishes. The most commonly mentioned traits in regards to parish vitality are the following: the number of registered families claiming parish membership; the number of active parishioners attending Mass on the weekends; the annual number of baptisms, funerals and marriages; the number of new parish members; the seating capacity of a church building; the condition of all parish buildings and the entire parish property; the number of existing parish ministries and available resources (both financial and manpower) to continue these ministries; parish

---

[112] Pope Francis, Address to the Faithful from the Diocese of Isernia-Venafro, The Vatican Radio, (May 02, 2015), Vatican, http://www.news.va/en/news/pope-parish-must-be-privileged-place-of-listening (accessed August 17, 2015).

financial stability and fiscal responsibility; and a parish outreach to a larger community.

A number of Church leaders in the United States have emphasized the need for accessing parish vitality in the context of the New Evangelization. One of the most recent diocesan resources regarding this subject was issued in 2010 by the Archdiocese of Washington, D.C. The title of this document is; *Indicators of Vitality. In Service of the New Evangelization.*[113] These practical and user-friendly guidelines emphasize the importance of evaluating parish vitality based on the following five core areas of parish life: worship, education, community, service, and administration. Cardinal Donald W. Wuerl, the archdiocesan shepherd, indicated the importance of this document in the opening remarks of his letter to the priests by stating:

As we carry out our pastoral service as priests, we recognize that for the most part the parish is the place where our ministry of word and sacrament unfolds. The parish is the community of faithful gathered with their pastor in the daily effort to respond to Jesus and his Gospel. You and I also realize that this is a time of challenge calling for a renewed evangelization reaching out to people living, as our Holy Father, Pope Benedict XVI, describes, "in a time of a progressive secularization of society and a kind of eclipse of the sense of God." The Pope calls us to a New Evangelization. The starting point for such an initiative is, as Pope John Paul II reminded us in *Ecclesia in America,* an encounter with the living Lord. The New Evangelization is not a program but rather a realization that we must re-propose the good news of the Gospel to a culture that really does not know Christ. For sure the light of Christ already shines brightly in each parish. Yet all of us recognize there is more to be done. Our archdiocesan efforts at a New Evangelization call us to look deeper into the vitality of our faith as it is expressed and lived in our parishes and in the homes of our people. Our Holy Father said in his meeting with the bishops of the United States during his visit here in Washington that even though the people of our country may appear to be very religious, "it is not enough for us to count on this traditional religiosity and go about business as usual." The evangelization that the Church envisions calls us to conversion and transformation, and in light of the culture we face we look to new methods of renewal and outreach.[114]

The five core areas of parish life and ministry have been further identified and explained for the benefit of pastors and lay faithful who find themselves in need of promoting an honest evaluation of parish vitality for the benefit of the entire church

---

[113] Archdiocese of Washington, D.C., *Indicators of Parish Vitality. In Service of the New Evangelization,* (Summer 2010), Washington, D.C., http://adw.org/wp-content/uploads/2014/02/ IOV Guide.pdf (accessed September 21, 2015).

[114] *Introductory Letter from the Archbishop, "Indicators of Vitality. In Service of the New Evangelization."*

community. Full and active participation of church members in the mission of the New Evangelization and the mission of their local parish requires first and foremost a candid assessment of the existing parish life, programs and ministries. If parish members are to become actively involved in the mission of the New Evangelization, they need to assess the present situation of their local parish in light of the following five fundamental elements for parish life and ministry:

Worship: The heart of parish life is the celebration of the Eucharist. From the Eucharist flows all of the worship, prayer and faith formation of the parish. This indicator examines the vitality of the parish's liturgical life.

Education: Forming the lay faithful for mission depends on a variety of educational programs. Assessing the parish's ability to provide education and faith formation to parishioners of all ages is the focus of this indicator.

Community: Building community begins with hospitality. Vitality is found in a parish's ability to make all members feel at home and to open wide the doors of the parish to welcome inactive Catholics and all who seek a relationship with the Lord.

Service: This dimension of parish life assesses the ways in which the parish calls parishioners to serve all those in need. It evaluates the parish's commitment to bring the Gospel to bear on the issues of the day in a way that supports the mission of the Church.

Administration: The ability to carry out the mission of the Church depends on strong leadership. In this area, staffing, management of parish resources and decision-making processes are evaluated.[115]

A strategic pastoral planning, an honest assessment of the current needs of a parish, and the development of a clear vision for the future are indispensable elements contributing to the formation of vibrant parishes which actively promote the call to the New Evangelization. A great number of lay and ordained church leaders who had written on this subject, are convinced that doing business as usual on a parish level will simply not suffice. There is a real danger in some parish communities as well as a temptation to fall into the self-preservation mode and to turn their churches and parish buildings into museums where the various artifacts of the previous glory days are being placed on display and admired. While church members must not ignore the history and the accomplishments of the past, they must also take an honest look at their parish ministries, activities and programs and assess whether or not these ministries and outreach are still relevant to the people of the twenty-first century and their needs.

There is a growing need in Catholic parishes of the new millennium to become centers of the New Evangelization. If Catholic parishes wish to have an

---

[115] *Indicators of Vitality. In Service of the New Evangelization*, 2.

important place in the lives of their members and potential converts, they need to assess and evaluate their ways of being a local church community in a highly secularized and consumeristic society. The constant call to conversion and the need to embrace the stewardship way of life must become an integral part of every parish community. This is the way for the Church of the new millennium if she wants to remain relevant in the lives of her people and the society as a whole. The message of the Gospel ought to be presented in new and more efficient ways aimed at touching and transforming the lives of all who hear it with their ears and hearts. Through the efforts of the New Evangelization, the local and Universal Church is called to a more fervent proclamation of the Kingdom of God that is here but not yet fully realized. Full and active participation of all Catholic faithful is absolutely essential in order to make local parishes vital centers of formation, witness and faith sharing.

The practical side of various pastoral plans providing criteria for parish vitality is that such strategies may be used to either develop a larger parish strategic vision for the future or they may be applied as evaluation tools for individual parish ministries. *The Indicators of Vitality* from the Archdiocese of Washington, D.C., have been written in both English and Spanish languages. In the process of doing so, they have become more accessible to the diverse Spanish-speaking Catholic communities living in the archdiocese. *The Indicators of Vitality* can be used in many other ways as well. The document suggests that they can be used as an assessment tool for the newly appointed pastor or as a platform for the future building and development of parish books and programs.[116]

The process of the New Evangelization calls upon all Catholic parishes to get actively involved in the mission of the Universal Church by proclaiming the teachings of the Gospel, by giving an authentic witness to Jesus Christ, by seeking the lost and by welcoming all who wish to become a part of a parish family. Promoting unity in diversity should be the guiding principle in this process. Enabling parish members to discover and to use their numerous gifts, talents and charisms for the benefit of the entire Body of Christ is an integral part of the New Evangelization and the formation of the missionary disciples. While implementing different assessment tools regarding parish vitality, it is imperative to have a task oriented and a mission-driven facilitator. Such facilitator must have the necessary skills to point out and present the most pressing parish goals as well as the methods and ways to achieve these targets in a timely manner. Skillful facilitators may be selected from the parish council members, from the parish community at large or from the diocesan staff members. Pastors and parish administrators may also serve as facilitators if they have the necessary skills and experience to carry this task.

Developing a list of parish strengths and weaknesses, prioritizing areas of immediate attention and development, listening to the parishioners and providing ways and means through which they can offer their input (written surveys, online tools and resources, town hall meetings), are also an integral part of the assessment

---

[116] *Indicators of Vitality. In Service of the New Evangelization*, 3.

process. Once a list of parish priorities has been developed including the long and short term goals and objectives along with the needed resources, the process of training and formation of parish members who will oversee different stages of implementation needs to take place. Specific groups or individuals should be put in charge as overseers of the implementation phase of this process. Developing a clear timeline and providing progress reports to the pastor, the parish council and members of the parish community will significantly advance the overall success of this life-giving and mission oriented endeavor. A parish self-study is an essential part of determining its viability. Frequent progress reports, transparency and an ongoing evaluation of achieved goals and progress are indispensable elements of the process aimed at assessing parish vitality.

Among the numerous pastoral plans in the United States regarding parish vitality, two plans from the Archdiocese of Philadelphia are of great importance: *Characteristics Found in Vital Parishes* and *In-Depth Evaluation of Parish Life.* The former document presents a different approach to the process of assessing parish vitality. Instead of evaluating the quantity, effectiveness and the variety of parish programs and ministries *Characteristics Found in Vital Parishes* proposes an assessment based on the parish support and involvement in the overall mission of the Church and her communion based on unity in diversity.

Vital and effective parishes are not determined principally on the basis of programs, no matter how successful. Programs allow for some degree of measurability but do not in themselves constitute parish vitality and effectiveness. Parish programs and ministries are the natural outgrowth of a clear understanding and commitment to the mission of the Church, supporting it and allowing true communion to flourish. This document, *Characteristics Found In Vital Parishes,* holds the hope that all involved in parish ministry, priests, deacons, religious, and laity alike, arrive at a common view of the parish's mission and how that mission is specifically and best lived out. It is this agreed upon mission, and the pastoral plan to accomplish it, that will determine the specific ministries, activities, and programs of each parish.[117]

The development of a clear parish mission and the promotion of continuous efforts aimed at deepening of the understanding of that mission are fundamental elements for parish existence and her evangelization efforts. Parish ministries, activities, programs and outreach must be deeply rooted in the mission of the local and universal church. Parish pastoral plans, goals, and visions for the future need to reflect and support the overall mission of the Universal Church. In the fall of 2011 the Archdiocese of Philadelphia released a hands-on document helping parishes to evaluate parish life in light of the mission of the entire Church. The document entitled; *In-Depth Evaluation of Parish Life,* discusses in detail the seven fundamental areas of parish life and ministry:

---

[117] Archdiocese of Philadelphia, *Characteristics Found in Vital Parishes,* (Spring 2003), 7, Philadelphia, http://archphila.org/pastplan/PDF/VitalParish.pdf (accessed September 21, 2015).

1. A Worshiping Parish: Prayer and Sacramental Life

2. A Welcoming and Caring Parish: Family and Community

3. A Witnessing and Proclaiming Parish: Invitation and Evangelization

4. An Educational and Formational Parish: Initiation and Faith Formation

5. A Parish Responsive to Others: Pastoral Outreach and Service for Justice

6. An Effectively Administered Parish: Leadership and Care of Facilities, Personnel and Finances

7. A Gifted Parish, Living Responsibly: Stewardship Formation and Practice.[118]

This important document underlines the importance of parish life and ministry on many different levels. Each parish community is portrayed in this resource as a worshipping community of faith where the diverse members celebrate the Eucharist together. It is a community where the parish members discover and nurture their call to become intentional missionary disciples. Catholic parishes are called to become places of welcome and warm hospitality where everybody can find a sense of belonging and genuine communion with God and with one another. Addressing the spiritual, personal and social needs of diverse parishioners needs to take place along with the formation of authentic witnesses and proclaimers of the Good News of the Gospel. Religious education and the spiritual formation of parish members need to be in the center of parish life and mission. In addition to addressing the needs of parish members Catholic parishes are also called to maintain a visible presence and an active involvement in the life of a larger civic community. Collaborative parish leadership based on delegation and recognition of multiple gifts and talents for the benefit of the entire faith community has been highly recommended as a very successful approach to parish governance and administration. In addition Catholic parishes have been entrusted with teaching and promoting the stewardship way of life as a disciple's response to a loving God who calls all of us to share our time, talent and treasure with others.

A Christian Steward is *one who receives God's gifts gratefully, cherishes and tends them in a responsible and accountable manner, shares them in justice and love with others, and returns them with increase to the Lord..* (United States Bishops. Pastoral Letter on Stewardship, November, 1992, Stewardship A Disciple's Response). The practice of Stewardship as a way of life is a basic ingredient for a flourishing parish faith community. The sense of shared responsibility for all aspects of parish life brings with it the commitment of

---

[118] Archdiocese of Philadelphia, *In-Depth Evaluation of Parish Life,* (Fall 2011), 2, Philadelphia, http://archphila.org/conversion/bulletin/BookletIndepthEvalofParishLife.pdf (accessed September 21, 2015).

time, talent and treasure…. Stewardship is a common thread linking Worship, Teaching, Christian Community, Christian Service, Evangelization and Leadership. Woven throughout everyday life, Stewardship makes known the mutual responsibility of one parishioner to the other as well as to the entire faith community.[119]

The topic of parish vitality has been addressed by numerous diocesan pastoral plans and letters containing helpful insights and tools regarding this subject. Below are just some of the most beneficial and user-friendly resources that may provide valuable assistance for parishes and dioceses in reference to the assessment of parish vitality: *In-Depth Evaluation of Parish Life* from the Archdiocese of Philadelphia, PA,[120] *Six Areas of Ministry Check List* from the Diocese of Davenport, IA,[121] *The Pastoral Plan for Parish Renewal and Restructuring; Attachment C:Criteria for Determining Parish Viability,* from the Diocese of Belleville, IL,[122] *Indicators of Parish Vitality,* from the Diocese of Rockford, IL,[123] *Hallmarks of Parish Vitality; A Self-Assessment Tool,* from the Diocese of Camden, NJ,[124] and from the Archdiocese of St. Louis, MO, *Parish Planning and Viability Study.*[125]

---

[119] Archdiocese of Philadelphia, *Characteristics Found in Vital Parishes,* (Spring 2003), 27, Philadelphia, http://archphila.org/pastplan/PDF/VitalParish.pdf (accessed September 21, 2015).

[120] Archdiocese of Philadelphia, *In-Depth Evaluation of Parish Life,* (Fall 2011), Philadelphia, http://archphila.org/conversion/bulletin/BookletIndepthEvalofParishLife.pdf (accessed September 15, 2015).

[121] Diocese of Davenport, IA, *Six Areas of Ministry Check List,* (August 29, 2014), Davenport, Iowa, http://www.davenportdiocese.org/library/Six%20Areas%20of%20Ministry%20Suggested%20Activities%208-29-14.pdf (accessed September 15, 2015).

[122] Diocese of Belleville, IL, *The Pastoral Plan for Parish Renewal and Restructuring; Attachment C:Criteria for Determining Parish Viability,* (June 8, 2014), Belleville, IL, http://www.diobelle.org/ documents/8Ccriteria.pdf (accessed September 15, 2015).

[123] Diocese of Rockford, IL, *Indicators of Parish Vitality,* (April 1997 and November 2010), Rockford, IL, https://www.rockforddiocese.org/pdfs/parishplanning/indicatorsofparishvitality.pdf (accessed September 15, 2015).

[124] Diocese of Camden, NJ, *Hallmarks of Parish Vitality; A Self-Assessment Tool,* (November 2012), Camden, NJ, http://www.google.com/url?sa=t&rct=j&q=&esrc=s&source=web&cd=4&cad=rja&uact=8&ved=0CC8QFjADahUKEwiBudTs6vnHAhWBNz4KHYDODLE&url=http%3A%2F%2Fharvestinggifts. Camden diocese.org%2Findex.php%2Fresources-by-discipline%2Fcategory%2F16-pastoralplanning%3Fdownload% 3D200%3Ahallmarks%2520of% 2520parish %2520vitality&usg=AFQjCNGeiunLRYc1-Sw8ktFdEvajcbbREg (accessed September 15, 2015).

[125] Archdiocese of St. Louis, MO, *Parish Planning and Viability Study,* (Spring 2015), St. Louis, MO, http://arch stl.org/files/field-file/STL%20Parish%20Planning%20and%20Viability%20Process%20(2).pdf (accessed September 15, 2015).

The Mission of the Church Universal and Local

When it comes to the subject of a parish mission, one should remember that such mission ought to flow from the mission of the Universal Church. The mission of a local church should reflect the overall mission of the Universal Church. Although parish mission statements may reflect important needs distinctively connected to a particular parish church community, the overall practice supporting the unity in diversity concept, has been that all local churches exemplify that diversified unity by sharing in the mission of the Universal Church. Therefore, the questions regarding the fundamental activity of the Church, as well as what she is supposed to be doing while existing here on earth, needs to be asked. What is the primary reason for the Church's existence? The fundamental activity/mission of the Church and the very reason for her existence is to proclaim the Gospel of Christ to all people and to give witness to it while being actively engaged in the making of the reality of the Kingdom of God present in our midst. Jesus Christ inaugurated the Kingdom of God on earth; however, that reality has not been yet fully accomplished. Therefore, it is the Church's mission to do everything that she can to help bring the Kingdom of God to its full realization.

> When Jesus, who had suffered the death of the cross for mankind, had risen, He appeared as the one constituted as Lord, Christ and eternal Priest, and He poured out on His disciples the Spirit promised by the Father. From this source the Church, equipped with the gifts of its Founder and faithfully guarding His precepts of charity, humility, and self-sacrifice, receives the mission to proclaim and to spread among all peoples the Kingdom of Christ and of God and to be, on earth, the initial budding forth of that kingdom. While it slowly grows, the Church strains toward the completed Kingdom and, with all its strength, hopes and desires to be united in glory with its King.[126]

The mission of the Church is the mission of Jesus Christ; "The Spirit of the Lord is upon me because he has anointed me to bring glad tidings to the poor. He has sent me to proclaim liberty to captives and recovery of sight to the blind, to let the oppressed go free, and to proclaim a year acceptable to the Lord." (Lk. 4:18-19) In addition, Jesus indicated that His mission to the world was to reach out to those in the world who have been lost so that they can have salvation in the full: "For the Son of Man has come to seek and to save what was lost." (Lk. 19:10) The mission of Jesus Christ is also the mission of God the Father who sent the Son so that all could be saved (Jn. 3:17) and that all could have a new life in abundance. (Jn. 10:10) The Church continues this Trinitarian mission through the power, guidance and the gifts of the Holy Spirit.

> The Son, therefore, came, sent by the Father. It was in Him, before the foundation of the world, that the Father chose us and predestined us to become adopted sons, for in Him it pleased the Father to re-establish all things. To

---

[126] *Lumen Gentium,* 5.

carry out the will of the Father, Christ inaugurated the Kingdom of heaven on earth and revealed to us the mystery of that kingdom. By His obedience, He brought about redemption. The Church, or, in other words, the kingdom of Christ now present in mystery, grows visibly through the power of God in the world…..When the work which the Father gave the Son to do on earth was accomplished, the Holy Spirit was sent on the day of Pentecost in order that He might continually sanctify the Church, and thus, all those who believe would have access through Christ in one Spirit to the Father. He is the Spirit of Life, a fountain of water springing up to life eternal. To men, dead in sin, the Father gives life through Him, until, in Christ, He brings to life their mortal bodies. The Spirit dwells in the Church and in the hearts of the faithful, as in a temple. In them, He prays on their behalf and bears witness to the fact that they are adopted sons. The Church, which the Spirit guides in way of all truth and which He unified in communion and in works of ministry, He both equips and directs with hierarchical and charismatic gifts and adorns with His fruits. By the power of the Gospel, He makes the Church keep the freshness of youth. Uninterruptedly He renews it and leads it to perfect union with its Spouse. The Spirit and the Bride both say to Jesus, the Lord, "Come!" Thus, the Church has been seen as "a people made one with the unity of the Father, the Son, and the Holy Spirit.[127]

The Holy Spirit sent at Pentecost lives in the Church both local and universal and continues to live in the hearts of the faithful. It is through the power, gifts and guidance of the Holy Spirit that the Church can continue her mission in the world. The Holy Spirit kindles the hearts of the faithful to go into the world and to evangelize through words and works. Their evangelizing efforts must reflect the great commission of Jesus Christ to "Go, therefore, and make disciples of all nations, baptizing them in the name of the Father, and of the Son, and of the holy Spirit, teaching them to observe all that I have commanded you. And behold, I am with you always, until the end of the age." (Mt. 28:19-20) It is through the workings of the Holy Spirit that new members are being received into the Church. It is the same Holy Spirit that calls the Church to a constant renewal while she continues to form a perfect union with her spouse Jesus Christ. The Church has been called by her founder to proclaim the Good News of the Gospel by word and sacrament. In a very special and unique way, the Church accomplishes this task through the celebration of the Eucharist that is the source and summit of Christian life.[128] The Christian life is fully realized in the celebration of the Eucharist and at the same time ordered towards it. The celebration of the Eucharist is also deeply connected with the mission of the Church.

> The liturgy (Eucharist) is the summit toward which the activity of the Church is directed; at the same time, it is the font from which all her power flows. For the aim and object of apostolic works is that all who are made sons of God by

---

[127] *Lumen Gentium*, 3-4.

[128] *Lumen Gentium*, 11.

faith and baptism should come together to praise God in the midst of His Church, to take part in the sacrifice, and to eat the Lord's supper.[129]

It is through the Eucharist that believers receive the strength for the journey ahead. At the same time, the celebration of the Eucharist should bring people to a closer relationship with God and with one another. Ultimately those who partake of the sacred meal are called to become what they receive – the Body of Christ. In addition to being the herald of the Word of God, the Church's mission in the world is to bear witness to the teachings of the Gospel that she proclaims. The mission of the Church must be the same as the mission of Jesus Christ. The Church must proclaim the teachings of her founder and the Good News of the Gospel for the salvation of all who are willing to embrace it and to follow it day in and day out. The kingdom of God has been inaugurated with the person and ministry of Jesus Christ. However, while the kingdom of God is here on earth, it has not yet reached its full maturity. Hence, some theologians will say that the kingdom of God is here but not yet fully realized.

Jesus of Nazareth brings God's plan to fulfillment. After receiving the Holy Spirit at his Baptism, Jesus makes clear his messianic calling: he goes about Galilee "preaching the Gospel of God and saying: 'The time is fulfilled, and the kingdom of God is at hand; repent and believe in the Gospel' (Mk 1: 14-15; cf. Mt 4: 17; Lk 4: 43). The proclamation and establishment of God's kingdom are the purpose of his mission: "I was sent for this purpose" (Lk 4: 43). But that is not all. Jesus himself is the "Good News," as he declares at the very beginning of his mission in the synagogue at Nazareth, when he applies to himself the words of Isaiah about the Anointed One sent by the Spirit of the Lord (cf. Lk 4: 14-21). Since the "Good News" is Christ, there is an identity between the message and the messenger, between saying, doing and being. His power, the secret of the effectiveness of his actions, lies in his total identification with the message he announces: he proclaims the "Good News" not just by what he says or does, but by what he is. The ministry of Jesus is described in the context of his journeys within his homeland. Before Easter, the scope of his mission was focused on Israel. Nevertheless, Jesus offers a new element of extreme importance. The eschatological reality is not relegated to a remote "end of the world," but is already close and at work in our midst. The kingdom of God is at hand (cf. Mk 1: 15); its coming is to be prayed for (cf. Mt 6: 10); faith can glimpse it already at work in signs such as miracles (cf. Mt 11: 4-5) and exorcisms (cf. Mt 12: 25-28), in the choosing of the Twelve (cf. Mk 3: 13-19), and in the proclamation of the Good News to the poor (cf. Lk 4: 18). Jesus' encounters with Gentiles make it clear that entry

---

[129] Second Vatican Ecumenical Council. The Constitution on the Sacred Liturgy *Sacrosanctum Concilium*, (December 4, 1963), 10, Vatican, http://www.vatican.va/archive/hist_councils/ii_vatican_council/ documents/vat-ii_const_19631204_sacrosanctum-concilium_en.html (accessed September 29, 2015). Here after cited as *Sacrosanctum Concilium*.

into the kingdom comes through faith and conversion (cf. Mk 1: 15), and not merely by reason of ethnic background. The kingdom which Jesus inaugurates is the kingdom of God. Jesus himself reveals who this God is, the One whom he addresses by the intimate term "Abba," Father (cf. Mk 14: 36). God, as revealed above all in the parables (cf. Lk 15: 3-32; Mt 20: 1-16), is sensitive to the needs and sufferings of every human being: he is a Father filled with love and compassion, who grants forgiveness and freely bestows the favors asked of him. St. John tells us that "God is love" (1 Jn 4: 8, 16). Every person, therefore, is invited to "repent" and to "believe" in God's merciful love.[130]

The kingdom of God is geared toward the transformation of human relationships as well as our relationship with God. Such transformation is possible when the followers of Jesus practice and experience love, forgiveness and compassion. However, none of this would be possible without the resurrection of Jesus. It is precisely because of the fact that Jesus died and rose to a new life that we have the promise of eternal life and the fulfillment of the kingdom of God that is yet to come.

The Resurrection gives a universal scope to Christ's message, his actions, and whole mission. The disciples recognize that the kingdom is already present in the person of Jesus and is slowly being established within man and the world through a mysterious connection with him. Indeed, after the Resurrection, the disciples preach the kingdom by proclaiming Jesus crucified and risen from the dead. In Samaria, Philip "preached good news about the kingdom of God and the name of Jesus Christ" (Acts 8: 12). In Rome, we find Paul "preaching the kingdom of God and teaching about the Lord Jesus Christ" (Acts 28: 31). The first Christians also proclaim "the kingdom of Christ and of God" (Eph 5: 5; cf. Rev 11: 15; 12: 10), or "the kingdom of our Lord and Savior Jesus Christ" (2 Pt 1: 11). The preaching of the early Church was centered on the proclamation of Jesus Christ, with whom the kingdom was identified. Now, as then, there is a need to unite the proclamation of the kingdom of God (the content of Jesus' own "kerygma") and the proclamation of the Christ-event (the "kerygma" of the apostles). The two proclamations are complementary; each throws light on the other….The kingdom cannot be detached either from Christ or from the Church. As has already been said, Christ not only proclaimed the kingdom, but in him the kingdom itself became present and was fulfilled. This happened not only through his words and his deeds: "Above all,…the kingdom is made manifest in the very person of Christ, Son of God and Son of Man, who came 'to serve and to give his life as a ransom for many' (Mk 10: 45)." The kingdom of God is not a concept, a doctrine, or a program subject to free interpretation, but it is before all else a person with the face and name of Jesus of Nazareth, the image of the invisible God. If the kingdom is separated from Jesus, it is no longer the kingdom of God which he revealed. The result is a distortion of the meaning of the kingdom, which runs

---

[130] *The Companion to the Catechism of the Catholic Church*, (San Francisco, CA: Ignatius Press, 1997), 365-366.

the risk of being transformed into a purely human or ideological goal, and a distortion of the identity of Christ, who no longer appears as the Lord to whom everything must one day be subjected (cf. 1 Cor 15: 27). [131]

The kingdom of God is fundamentally connected with the person and mission of Jesus Christ. Jesus proclaimed the kingdom of God and inaugurated its fulfillment. Furthermore, since Jesus himself founded the Church and entrusted her with a specific mission to make the reality of the kingdom of God present in our midst, the Church is inseparably linked to both the kingdom of God and her spouse Jesus Christ.

Likewise, one may not separate the kingdom from the Church. It is true that the Church is not an end unto herself since she is ordered towards the kingdom of God of which she is the seed, sign, and instrument. Yet, while remaining distinct from Christ and the kingdom, the Church is indissolubly united to both. Christ endowed the Church, his Body, with the fullness of the benefits and means of salvation. The Holy Spirit dwells in her, enlivens her with his gifts and charisms, sanctifies, guides and constantly renews her. The result is a unique and special relationship which, while not excluding the action of Christ and the Spirit outside the Church's visible boundaries, confers upon her a specific and necessary role; hence the Church's special connection with the kingdom of God and of Christ, which she has "the mission of announcing and inaugurating among all peoples." It is within this overall perspective that the reality of the kingdom is understood. [132]

While the Church is not to be mistakenly perceived as the total fulfillment of the kingdom of God, she is a sign of the kingdom of God and also a proclaimer of its values expressed by the promotion of peace, justice, liberty and compassion. In other words, the Church is called to an authentic witness and the promotion of faithful discipleship based on the teachings and the proclamation of the Good News of the Gospel.

The Church is effectively and concretely at the service of the kingdom. This is seen especially in her preaching, which is a call to conversion. Preaching constitutes the Church's first and fundamental way of serving the coming of the kingdom in individuals and in human society. Eschatological salvation begins even now in newness of life in Christ: "To all who believed in him, who believed in his name, he gave power to become children of God" (Jn 1: 12). The Church, then, serves the kingdom by establishing communities and founding new particular churches, and by guiding them to mature faith and charity in openness towards others, in service to individuals and society, and in understanding and esteem for human institutions. The Church serves the kingdom by spreading throughout the world the "Gospel values" which are an

---

[131] *The Companion to the Catechism of the Catholic Church*, (San Francisco, CA: Ignatius Press, 1997), 367-368.

[132] Ibid., 368.

58

expression of the kingdom and which help people to accept God's plan. It is true that the inchoate reality of the kingdom can also be found beyond the confines of the Church among peoples everywhere, to the extent that they live "Gospel values" and are open to the working of the Spirit who breathes when and where he wills (cf. Jn 3: 8). But it must immediately be added that this temporal dimension of the kingdom remains incomplete unless it is related to the kingdom of Christ present in the Church and straining towards eschatological fullness. The many dimensions of the kingdom of God do not weaken the foundations and purposes of missionary activity, but rather strengthen and extend them. The Church is the sacrament of salvation for all mankind, and her activity is not limited only to those who accept her message. She is a dynamic force in mankind's journey towards the eschatological kingdom and is the sign and promoter of Gospel values. The Church contributes to mankind's pilgrimage of conversion to God's plan through her witness and through such activities as dialogue, human promotion, commitment to justice and peace, education and the care of the sick, and aid to the poor and to children. In carrying on these activities, however, she never loses sight of the priority of the transcendent and spiritual realities which are premises of eschatological salvation. Finally, the Church serves the kingdom by her intercession, since the kingdom by its very nature is God's gift and work, as we are reminded by the Gospel parables and by the prayer which Jesus taught us. We must ask for the kingdom, welcome it and make it grow within us; but we must also work together so that it will be welcomed and will grow among all people, until the time when Christ "delivers the kingdom to God the Father" and "God will be everything to everyone" (cf. 1 Cor 15: 24, 28). 854 (1) *Redemptoris missio* 42-47 People today put more trust in witnesses than in teachers, in experience than in teaching, and in life and action than in theories. The witness of a Christian life is the first and irreplaceable form of mission: Christ, whose mission we continue, is the "witness" par excellence (Rev 1: 5; 3: 14) and the model of all Christian witness. The Holy Spirit accompanies the Church along her way and associates her with the witness he gives to Christ (cf. Jn 15: 26-27). The first form of witness is the very life of the missionary, of the Christian family, and of the ecclesial community, which reveal a new way of living. The missionary, who, despite all his or her human limitations and defects, lives a simple life, taking Christ as the model, is a sign of God and of transcendent realities. But everyone in the Church, striving to imitate the Divine Master, can and must bear this kind of witness; in many cases it is the only possible way of being a missionary.[133]

While the Church calls others through her proclamation and witness to an ongoing conversion in light of the teachings of the Gospel, she must continually strive to reform and renew her own structures and the methods employed in her mission. Above all the Church is at the service of the kingdom of God. She exists for the sake

[133] *The Companion to the Catechism of the Catholic Church*, (San Francisco, CA: Ignatius Press, 1997), 368-369.

of making the reality of God's kingdom present in our midst through her unbiased proclamation of the Gospel to all people and all nations. The Church should be a sign and an instrument of the kingdom of God while preaching the Good News of the Gospel and giving witness to it. As a sign and instrument of God's kingdom and that of the Gospel the fundamental part of the mission of the Church is to engage the society actively in the promotion of social justice, her defense of human life and dignity and her protection of the poor, the hungry and the marginalized. The Church just like every one of her members is called to an ongoing conversion in order to build up the kingdom of God for the salvation of all.

> The kingdom will grow insofar as every person learns to turn to God in the intimacy of prayer as to a Father (cf. Lk 11: 2; Mt 23: 9) and strives to do his will (cf. Mt 7: 21). Jesus gradually reveals the characteristics and demands of the kingdom through his words, his actions, and his own person. The kingdom of God is meant for all mankind, and all people are called to become members of it. To emphasize this fact, Jesus drew especially near to those on the margins of society and showed them a special favor in announcing the Good News. At the beginning of his ministry, he proclaimed that he was "anointed . . . to preach good news to the poor" (Lk 4: 18). To all who are victims of rejection and contempt, Jesus declares: "Blessed are you poor" (Lk 6: 20). What is more, he enables such individuals to experience liberation even now, by being close to them, going to eat in their homes (cf. Lk 5: 30; 15: 2), treating them as equals and friends (cf. Lk 7: 34), and making them feel loved by God, thus revealing his tender care for the needy and for sinners (cf. Lk 15: 1-32)…The kingdom aims at transforming human relationships; it grows gradually as people slowly learn to love, forgive and serve one another. Jesus sums up the whole Law, focusing it on the commandment of love (cf. Mt 22: 34-40; Lk 10: 25-28). Before leaving his disciples, he gives them a "new commandment:" "Love one another; even as I have loved you" (Jn 13: 34; cf. 15: 12). Jesus' love for the world finds its highest expression in the gift of his life for mankind (cf. Jn 15: 13), which manifests the love which the Father has for the world (cf. Jn 3: 16). The kingdom's nature, therefore, is one of communion among all human beings—with one another and with God. The kingdom is the concern of everyone: individuals, society, and the world. Working for the kingdom means acknowledging and promoting God's activity, which is present in human history and transforms it. Building the kingdom means working for liberation from evil in all its forms. In a word, the kingdom of God is the manifestation and the realization of God's plan of salvation in all its fullness. By raising Jesus from the dead, God has conquered death, and in Jesus he has definitely inaugurated his kingdom. During his earthly life, Jesus was the Prophet of the kingdom; after his Passion, Resurrection and Ascension into heaven he shares in God's power and in his dominion over the world (cf. Mt 28: 18; Acts 2: 36; Eph 1: 18-21).[134]

[134] *The Companion to the Catechism of the Catholic Church*, (San Francisco, CA: Ignatius Press, 1997), 365-366.

The mission of Jesus must be reflected in the mission of the Universal Church. Furthermore, the mission of the Universal Church must be reflected in the mission statements of local parishes. While diversified parish communities have the right to respond effectively to the different needs of local communities, Catholic parishes are also called to proclaim the Gospel of Jesus Christ by words, the celebration of sacraments and by their witness. Local parishes are called to become centers of the New Evangelization where the missionary disciples are being formed and where the Word of God is alive in the hearts of the faithful. In order to create such centers, present day Catholic parishes need to evaluate their vitality and faithfulness to their mission statements. Changes and adjustments in parish missions need to reflect the current needs of a community of faith and the overall needs of a local community. Several different authors emphasize the need for Catholic parishes to move the focus of their attention from maintenance to mission if they wish to remain relevant in the lives of their members and the community at large.

> All organizations need mission if they are to stay healthy. Organizational development theory tells us that healthy organizations are ones that have a clear sense of mission. Low morale results from the aimlessness and malaise that come from the lack of mission. When we have a clear outward focus, some of our internal problems tend to fall into perspective. When we are not absorbed by the mission, these internal problems are magnified. When we do have an outward missionary focus, our problems diminish in importance because we identify with and seek to do something about suffering in the world. In adopting a missionary rather than a maintenance approach, parishes are not only being faithful to the mandate of Christ, but they also find a remedy for the malaise that comes from excessive focus on their internal dissensions.[135]

A clear and concise mission of the parish should become the driving force behind all ministries, parish programs and activities. Most of all, Catholic parishes and their members ought to become actively involved in the local and universal Church efforts aimed at the New Evangelization. The lay faithful, the ordained and the religious members of the Church are called to become intentional disciples who actively engage in making the mission of Jesus Christ and his Church being presently realized in this world through the proclamation of the Gospel and an authentic Christian witness. In order to make this mission a reality, Catholic parishes need to enter into a dialogue with the modern world and culture. This dialogue, in order to be most effective, ought to be based on openness, respect for the opposite points of view, and sensitivity toward ethnic, socio-economic and cultural diversities. Interreligious dialogue is recommended as one of the ways in the process of creating a more holistic, just, and Gospel-oriented society. An ongoing ecumenical dialogue is an integral part of the Church's mission.

---

[135] Robert S. Rivers, CSP, *From Maintenance to Mission: Evangelization and the Revitalization of the Parish* (Mahwah, New Jersey: Paulist Press, 2014), 23.

Evangelization is the basic duty of the whole people of God. Therefore, the responsibility for the mission will be born today and in the future not only by priests and religious orders but more than previously by lay people. Because of their baptism and confirmation, they want to bear witness to Jesus Christ in their respective environment and be 'salt of the earth' (Mt. 5.13f.) They can let themselves be sent out temporarily or permanently to contribute their knowledge and expertise as craftsmen and professionals, as teachers, doctors, and nurses, as engineers, as business advisors and many more and thereby profess their faith as Christians…Finally, and above all, the mission in the present and the future will be shaped by the spirit dialogue with indigenous religions and cultures, by the effort for inculturation, and by the preferential option for the poor. In other words, it will be holistic and combined with the fight against injustice and oppression, persecution, poverty, hunger, and illness as well as with furthering a whole human culture. In the light of common challenges for all Christians, the mission cannot happen in competition with other churches and ecclesial communities but wherever and as far as possible in ecumenical cooperation.[136]

Essential Elements for the Process of Merging, Closing and Collaborating of Catholic Parishes.

Every parish community no matter how large or small ought to have a clear and easy to remember mission statement. The mission statement of every parish should reflect the core elements of their Christian identity and specific ways in which they realize their call to discipleship. In addition, to the mission statement describing who we are as an ecclesial community, every parish should have a vision for the future. If we do not know who we are and where we are going, then how can we effectively and enthusiastically fulfill Jesus' great commission; "Go, therefore, and make disciples of all nations, baptizing them in the name of the Father, and of the Son, and of the Holy Spirit, teaching them to observe all that I have commanded you. And behold, I am with you always, until the end of the age."[137] Church communities that lack mission and vision tend to focus their attention more on self-preservation and business as usual mentality. Dying parishes quite often become absorbed with the preservation of buildings rather than creating a welcoming church community that offers quality ministries, programs, and services. Mission oriented Catholic parishes acknowledge the dual aspects of their mission: reaching out to their respective members but also serving the needs of the wider community. Churches and parishes are a part of their local neighborhoods. They are an integral part of cities and villages where the Catholic faithful live and function. When Catholic parishes no longer provide any kind of outreach to the larger community, they tend to become self-centered and self-serving. When a parish church becomes a fortress guarded by the diehard guards and when parish membership is perceived as being a part of an elitist

[136] Walter Kasper, *The Catholic Church: Nature, Reality and Mission* (London: Bloomsbury, T&T Clark, 2015), 293-294.
[137] Mt. 28:19-20.

and exclusive private club, there is hardly any room left for proclaiming Christ and his Gospel.

Catholic parishes should make the time to do an honest evaluation of parish programs, outreach, ministries, organizations and provided services. In short, every Catholic parish should engage in a detailed assessment of parish life and vibrancy. This commendable practice ought to become a starting point for parish mergers, closures, and collaborations. Depending on individual circumstances, Catholic parishes should perform an evaluation of parish vibrancy at least once every three years. Parish leaders and parishioners ought to be willing to check whether or not they have been faithful to their mission and vision. If either one of them has changed in the last few years then maybe there is a need for some adjustments in order to best serve the needs of the people. Catholic parishes which find themselves going through structural changes that involve merging, closing or collaboration, could greatly benefit from an honest evaluation of the state of their parish unions. When parishioners are well informed about the strengths and the possible future challenges that their church community may experience, they may be more willing and accepting to participate in the process aimed at introducing parish structural changes.

One of the most crucial elements for any process involving merging, closing or collaborating of parishes is communication. From the early planning stages of the process until the development of a final plan and its implementation, ongoing communication between the diocese, the parishes involved, parish members and leaders is absolutely indispensable. The rule of thumb for pastors and parish leaders should be: communicate often and communicate adequate information. While the sharing of information is essential for the success of the process, honesty and transparency must accompany it as well. Consistency in regards to the conveyed message must also be taken into consideration. All parties involved must hear the same message. Otherwise, unnecessary rumors and half-truths will spread like wildfires and negatively impact the process. An open dialogue between all parties involved must be the guiding principle in this process as well. Facts and hard truths affecting parish life and ministries need to be fully disclosed so that all parish members will understand the reasons behind the structural changes. All voices must be heard no matter how painful or how brutally honest. The people in the pews should never be treated as passive recipients of the sacraments. They are the living and breathing Body of Christ. They are the face of God among us and they deserve to be treated with respect and pastoral sensitivity. The voice of the lay faithful must never be underestimated. They have much to share and to offer, and church leaders ought to learn how to listen attentively to their diverse voices. Appropriate forums must be created in order to provide numerous opportunities to hear the voice of the people and to let them express their fears, dreams, and hopes.

Those parish members whose churches may cease to exist need to be provided with ways and means to grieve their loss and to express their sorrows. Many present-day writers on the subject emphasize the importance and the need to ritualize those important milestones and transitions in the life of a parish. The transfer of religious art effects and especially the transfer of the Blessed Sacrament have been done in some parishes in a form of a procession to the "new church," where it was witnessed and welcomed by all parishioners of the newly formed parish. No parish transition or structural change can ever be successful without developing a parish culture of sincere hospitality and warm welcome. People involved in the process must have the assurance that this is not about us joining them or vice versa. This process is about coming together as one, recognizing each others' gifts and working together for the benefit of all. A parish church should become a true spiritual home for the many diverse members who come together as one and who realize their call of becoming intentional disciples. Parish mergers, closures, and collaboration, can be life giving or life taking. Parish and diocesan leaders who oversee such transitions ought to make sure that the reasons behind the parish structural changes are well explained and understood by all parties involved.

Last but not least, consultation, flexibility and openness to compromise should be the guiding factors for parish mergers, closures, and collaborations. When everything appears to be written in stone, and there isn't the slightest opportunity for additional discussion and proposals, people in the pews and parish leaders may be under the impression that they were just going through the motions while the final decision had already been made. They need to know that their input is valued and appreciated. Parish structural changes should be introduced in a timely manner. The process of merging, closing and collaborating of Catholic parishes should not be prolonged over an indefinite period of time nor should it be rushed too quickly. A clear timeline with a task list ought to accompany any such a process. In doing so, the participants will continue to receive information about the progress being made and the specific goals being accomplished.

The Catholic Parish in Canon Law

Juridic Person

For a great majority of people who are members of the Roman Catholic Church as well as for those outside of the Catholic culture and Church structure the terms: *juridic person* or *juridical person* may come across as something foreign and not very easily understood. For canon lawyers and people who use and apply the 1983 Code of Canon Law on a regular basis *a juridic person* or *juridical personality* indicates that such an entity is a subject to the rights and obligations as prescribed by the norms and regulations of the Code of Canon Law. In other words, the terms *juridic person* or *juridic persons* is considered to be an aggregate of persons or things.

> Juridic personality is a concept linked to how the law views an individual. If the law recognizes an individual as a subject of rights and duties, then we can say they possess juridic personality. The concept of a parish being accorded juridic personality is simply recognition that the parish is treated by the law as

a subject of rights and duties. This status is, perhaps, more readily understandable for individual human beings. Canon 96, for example, establishes that 'a human being is incorporated by baptism in the Church of Christ and constituted a person in it, with the duties and rights which are proper to Christians, according to their condition, inasmuch as they are in ecclesiastical communion and not impeded by a sanction legitimately imposed.' A juridic person, however, is an aggregate, which is acknowledged by the law as a subject of rights and duties, i e, possessing juridic personality. In canon law, these juridic persons can be aggregates of persons or things (can. 115 §1), public or private (can. 116 §1). An ecclesiastical juridic person is the product of a juridic act by the competent authority of the Church. According to can. 116: *Public juridical persons are aggregates of persons or of things which are constituted by the competent ecclesiastical authority so that, within the limits allotted to them, they might in the name of the Church and in accordance with the provisions of law, fulfill the specific task entrusted to them in view of the public good. Public juridical persons are given this personality either by the law itself or by a special decree of the competent authority expressly granting it.* The public juridical person, then, is a creature of the Church. It is an entity created within the Church by the decisive choice of the Church. It is created precisely to act, to fulfill a specific task that is entrusted to it ...*in the name of the Church*. They are directed to a purpose befitting the Church's mission, which concerns works of piety, the apostolate or charity, whether spiritual or temporal, and which transcends the purpose of the individuals (can. 114 §§1-2). According to the provisions of the Code of Canon Law there are basically, two, and only two ways that juridic personality may be acquired: either from the law itself, or by special decree of the competent authority expressly granting it.[138]

Some entities receive the status of a juridic personality based on the Law itself. The Church's law, for example, recognizes dioceses (can. 368), parishes (can. 515§3), seminaries (can. 238§1), religious institutes, provinces and houses (can. 634§1), as public ecclesiastical juridic persons. Other aggregates of persons or things may obtain the status of a juridic person "only by the special decree of competent ecclesiastical authority (can. 116§2."[139] Granting the status of a juridic person can also be applied to Catholic hospitals, schools, associations and non-profit institutions that are affiliated with the Catholic Church. However, for the juridic personality to be granted by an appropriate ecclesiastical authority, various aggregates must clearly specify the purpose of their existence (can. 114§3). Furthermore, they must provide the means of achieving such a purpose and be governed by statutes and constitutions aimed at the fulfillment of its mission which is the very reason for their existence (can. 94). A Catholic parish comes into existence once a diocesan bishop issues a decree of erection (can. 515§2) in accordance with the norms of Canon Law. Canon

---

[138] Thomas A. Baima, ed. *What is a Parish? Canonical, Pastoral, and Theological Perspectives* (Chicago, IL: Liturgy Training Publications, 2011), 59-60.

[139] Ibid., 60.

515§3 indicates that the juridic personality of a legitimately erected parish comes from the law itself.

> Once a parish has been legitimately erected it possesses juridic personality by law itself. The parish considered as a juridic person is the entity created by the juridic act of the bishop erecting it as a parish. Theoretically, the community may disperse, but the parish, as a juridic person, will continue to exist until it is extinguished according to the norms of law: i.e., either by decree of legitimate authority or by cessation of all activity for a period of one hundred years (can. 120§1). The juridic personality is not granted by the diocesan bishop, though he alone has competence to erect (suppress or notably alter) a parish. A juridic person is a subject in canon law of obligations and rights which correspond to its nature (can. 113§2); by its nature, every juridic person is perpetual (can. 120§1). The parish is a public juridic person (can. 116). It is a non-collegial *universitas personarum,* that is, a *universitas* whose members do not determine its actions through common decision making (can. 115§2). The pastor alone represents it in all juridic affairs according to the norm of law; he is to take care that parochial goods are administered according to the norm of canons 1281-1288 (can. 532; see can. 118).[140]

The Rights and Obligations of a Parish and its Members

In accordance with the norms of the law being a *juridic person* a Catholic parish has certain rights and obligations which are listed implicitly and explicitly in the 1983 Code of Canon Law. The law governing the Catholic Church makes a very specific and detailed mention of the rights and obligations of the Catholic faithful as individual members of the Church. The so-called "bill of rights" covers a wide variety of rights and obligations pertaining to all the baptized members of the Church. The rights and obligations of all the Christian faithful are listed in canons 208–223. Moreover, the Code of Canon Law mentions specific rights and obligations of the three groups of people who fall under the category of all baptized Christians: laity (canons 224-231), clergy (canons 273-289) and religious (canons 662-672). When it comes to Catholic parishes, the rights and obligations are mentioned throughout the Code of Canon Law both explicitly and implicitly. As local church communities, Catholic parishes ought to be understood as Eucharistic communities comprised of the baptized Christian faithful who are in communion with one another and with the diocesan and universal church. Local Catholic church communities enjoy a certain degree of freedom in various areas of parish life, ministry, and service. Catholic parishes are authentic Christian churches that realize the mission of Christ in our midst. However, in regards to parish governance, Catholic parishes fall under the canonical jurisdiction of a local diocesan bishop who appoints a parish pastor and who has the final say according to the norms of the law. If Catholic parishes are to

---

[140] John P. Beal, James A. Coriden, and Thomas J. Green, ed. *New Commentary on the Code of Canon Law* (New York, N.Y./Mahwah, N.J: Paulist Press, 2000), 680-681.

fulfill their mission and to become effective centers of the New Evangelization and formation of intentional disciples, the principle of subsidiarity must be taken into account.

1. The church in its most authentic reality is a communion of churches. It is built up from below by local congregations that are in communion with one another. At every level, the church is a communion of communities. The dignity and legitimate autonomy of local churches must be affirmed, especially in these times of strong centralizing tendencies, and the assertion of their rights and obligations is one important way of doing that.

2. The principle of subsidiarity function insists that the internal life of local communities must be respected and not usurped or dominated from outside. This applies to parishes and other congregations, and one way of demonstrating that is by focusing on their rights and duties.[141]

Parish rights and obligations are listed and implied in several places throughout the code. The Code of Canon Law acknowledges that a diocese is to be divided into distinct parts or parishes (canon 374, §1). Catholic parishes are to be understood as communities of the Christian faithful stably constituted within a territory of a particular church, whose pastoral care is given to a parish pastor (proper pastor) under the authority of the diocesan bishop (canon 515, §1). The law recognizes parishes as public juridic persons (515, §3) with a right to owe property. Parishes have a right and an obligation to maintain communion with other ecclesiastical communities (canon 209) and with the Universal Church. In addition, members of Catholic parishes have the right to equality in dignity and action (canon 208) and the right to hear the word of God and to celebrate the sacraments (canon 213), and the right to pastoral ministry and leadership (canons 515, §1, 516, §2, 517, §2). Moreover, parish members have the right to initiate and sustain activities and services, the right to association and assembly, (canons 211, 215-216, 298-299). Furthermore, parish members have the right to information, communication and consultation (canons 212, §2, 212, §3) and the right to formation and education (canons 217, 788, 789, 793-798, 800 and 851). Additionally, parishioners have the right and obligation to evangelize and support the mission of the Church (canons 211 and 781), the right to sanctification and spiritual growth (canons 210 and 770). Catholic parishes have the right to own and to use goods and property (canons 1255-1256). Parishes also have the right and obligation to vindicate and defend their rights in the same manner that the individual Christian faithful (all baptized) have the right to defend their rights (canon 221, §1).[142]

While these rights and obligations specify the role, mission, and purpose as well as the rules of governance for Catholic parishes, these laws also have their limitations. James A. Coriden recognizes these limitations on three different levels:

---

[141] James A. Coriden, *The Parish in Catholic Tradition: History, Theology, and Canon Law* (Mahwah, N.J: Paulist Press, 1997), 72.

[142] James A. Coriden, *The Parish in Catholic Tradition: History, Theology, and Canon Law* (Mahwah, N.J: Paulist Press, 1997), 72-81.

by circumstances, by the rights of others and by the common good.[143] Catholic parishes live and function in the world and as such they are being influenced and affected by different factors and circumstances (socio-economic conditions and political systems, as well as cultural, local and universal factors). While applying and exercising canonical rights and obligations, one must take into consideration factors such as the common good of all, justice, fairness, the respect for the rights of others and the good of the whole Church. It is also worth remembering that local parishes are authentic church communities which relate to other local church communities and continue to foster a relationship with the diocesan and the Universal Church. These unique relationships between the local, the particular and the universal church are based on unity in diversity which ultimately leads to the formation of a real and visible communion of churches.

The Legal Agents Claiming Parish Rights and Obligations.

Having mentioned various rights and obligations pertaining to Catholic parishes and their members, the next important steps are aimed to determine who can claim these rights and how can they be claimed? Understanding the Catholic Church as a community of communities is of great importance in order to comprehend how her governing law is interpreted, applied and executed when it comes to the subject of local parishes and their rights and obligations. In accordance with the provisions of the Code of Canon Law, the proper pastor of a parish can vindicate and defend parish rights and obligations. He is the proper shepherd of souls entrusted with the authority to act on behalf of a parish understood as a public juridic person. The proper pastor acts on behalf of a parish in all legal, financial and administrative matters in accordance with the norm of the law (canon 532).

In case of a diocese, it is the diocesan bishop who acts as juridic representative for a particular church entrusted to his canonical jurisdiction (canon 381, §1). When it comes to the Universal Church, it is the Roman Pontiff who acts on her behalf and who represents her in accordance with the norms of the law (canon 332, §1). The Canon Law also states that a pastor must possess the stability of office (canon 522), which when properly applied provides a sense of permanency and continuity for the Catholic faithful entrusted into his pastoral care. Some people could argue that the pastor is the proper guardian, protector, and defender of a parish community. He is also the juridic administrator of temporal goods connected with a parish community. In short the pastor is the legal representative of the public juridic person – the parish.

> The public juridic person *acts* through persons designated in accord with Church law and its own statutes to represent it or to act in its name. Those who are so designated act either collegially or not in accord with the law and the statutes of the juridic person (cf. can. 115§2, 119 and 127). These are the persons who are, with respect to the conditions necessary for the validity of a juridical act, *legally capable of acting* for the juridic person, capable of

---

[143] Ibid., 80.

committing the juridic person to an obligation. When they act on behalf of the juridic person, they necessarily are performing juridic acts. When the law or the statutes of the juridic person requires this capable person or "superior" to obtain the consent or the advice of others to perform juridic act, it must be considered a legal *requisite for the validity* of the act. In the case of a parish, the person who acts for the parish in juridic matters is the priest-pastor.[144]

The pastor of the parish is the proper shepherd and the one to whom the pastoral care of souls has been entrusted under the authority of the diocesan bishop (canon 519). The pastor of the church in cooperation with the lay and ordained members of that church is to exercise his threefold ministry: to teach, to sanctify and to govern. In accordance with the norms of the law the pastor represents the parish in all juridic, financial and administrative affairs (canon 532). While acting on behalf of the parish, the pastor must adhere to the norms regarding the temporal goods which are contained in canons 1281-1288. In addition to the pastor (canon 532), his substitutes (parochial administrators canon 540, §1) and parochial vicars (canon 541), are recognized by Canon Law as other agents and entities capable of defending and vindicating parish rights and obligations. Among those other agents capable of vindicating parish rights the provisions of the Code of Canon Law recognize *several priests in solidium* (jointly) where one of them serves as the moderator (canons 517, §1, 520, §1, 526, §2 and 527, §2) who alone represents the parish in juridic affairs (canon 543, §2,3). Furthermore, the pastoral care of the parish may be entrusted to a deacon, a lay person and a community of persons (canon 517, §2). However, in the cases mentioned above, it is the responsibility of the diocesan bishop to appoint a priest overseer who possesses the powers and faculties of a pastor. While persons other than the proper pastor may participate in the pastoral care of the parish, they do not exercise the full care of souls which is reserved only to an ordained priest (canon 150).

> The fact that the parish is entrusted to a priest-pastor, who is its proper shepherd, helps clergy and faithful to understand the sacred relationship that exists between priests and people. It is a relationship that is certainly under the authority of the diocesan bishop, but it also establishes a realm that is proper to the priest-pastor as well. While there are still those who misunderstand the significance of the share in the pastoral care that can be given to deacons and non-ordained faithful (cf. can.517, §2), bishops and canonists included, the priest-pastor possesses an ontological sacramentally based share in exercising the functions of teaching, sanctifying and governing in the person of Christ, the Head of the Church, which cannot be validly given to a person who is not an ordained priest. This is not a simple issue of bureaucracy or law. It touches on the very nature of the sacramental hierarchical priesthood. What each of these components of the legal architecture of the parish demonstrate is how

---

[144] Thomas A. Baima, ed. *What is a Parish? Canonical, Pastoral, and Theological Perspectives* (Chicago, IL: Liturgy Training Publications, 2011), 61.

69

carefully balanced are all the ecclesiological roles that intersect at this grass roots level of living the faith in the Church and in the world.[145]

In addition to these immediate agents claiming parish rights and obligations there are other groups such as the parish pastoral council (canon 536), the parish finance council (canon 537) and the parishioners at large. The recent practice of the highest court of the Catholic Church, the Apostolic Signatura, indicates that at least one parish member in good standing is needed to vindicate and defend parish rights.[146] Moreover, other people and entities such as church officials - deans (canon 555), episcopal vicars, presbyteral councils (canons 495, §1, 515, §2, 1222, §2), the promoter of justice (canon 1430), the vicar general and the diocesan bishop - should also share in the duty and responsibility of vindicating parish rights and obligations.[147]

The Ways and Methods of Vindicating Parish Rights and Obligations.

Those entrusted with the responsibility of vindicating parish rights and obligations ought to make sure that they possess all and any necessary information, documents, plans, reviews, reports and assessments which affect the life and interests of the parish. In cases where there is a clear notion supported by indisputable evidence that parish rights have been violated or infringed upon, the legal agents acting on behalf of the parish may seek conciliation, mediation or they can make a direct appeal to the proper ecclesiastical authority (canons 1713-1716). There is always an option to initiate an administrative recourse of appeal either to the author of the decision or to their ecclesiastical superior (canons 1732-1739). The petitioner must state his/her appeal in writing within the allotted period of time (ten days for the first appeal, canon 1734, §2), during which time the proposed decree in question is suspended. The author of the decree or decision has thirty days to amend the decision, to issue a new decree or to reject the petition (canon 1735).

The petitioner who feels aggrieved by a decree has the right to appeal directly to the ecclesiastical superior of the author of the decree. In the case of diocesan bishops, it is the Vatican Congregation for Clergy which handles such appeals. When everything else fails, the petitioner has the right to make a direct appeal to the supreme tribunal of the Catholic Church, the Apostolic Signatura (canon 1445, §2). In accordance with canon 221, the Christian faithful have the right to claim and defend their rights and obligations through the ecclesiastical courts.

---

[145] Thomas A. Baima, ed. *What is a Parish? Canonical, Pastoral, and Theological Perspectives* (Chicago, IL: Liturgy Training Publications, 2011), 65-66.

[146] James A. Coriden, *The Parish in Catholic Tradition: History, Theology, and Canon Law* (Mahwah, N.J: Paulist Press, 1997), 85-86.

[147] Ibid., 86.

The Canonical Requirements and Process for Parish Closures and Mergers.

The closures and mergers of Catholic parishes have become an undeniable reality affecting many dioceses in the United States and around the world (Scotland, Ireland, England, and Germany). In the United States, this alarming trend has been especially visible in the Midwest and Northeast parts of the country. According to the Center for Applied Research in the Apostolate (CARA) and its Nineteen Sixty-four research blog edited by Mark. M. Gray, during the last fourteen years (2000-2014), the number of parish affiliated Catholics has grown by 11% and the number of self-identified Catholics has grown by 7% (five million people). However, during the same time period the number of Catholic parishes in the United States has declined by 1,753 parishes (-9%). Furthermore, between 2000 and 2014 the number of active priests has fallen by 7,424 (-16%). Moreover, the number of parishes without a resident priest pastor has increased by 653 to the total of 3,496 (+ 23%).

> The Catholic Church in the U.S. has experienced a net loss of 1,753 parishes since 2000 (-9%). Most of these losses have occurred in the Northeast and Midwest with too few parishes being opened in the South and West where Catholic population growth is concentrated. Although ordinations are up, these remain insufficient to maintain the population of priests due to retirements and deaths. Overall, the number of priests in the U.S. has fallen by 7,424 since 2000 (-16%). The number of parishes without a resident priest pastor has increased by 653 to 3,496 (+23%). The ratio of active diocesan priests to parishes has decreased from 1.2 to a precarious 1.0. Although more parishes are without a resident priest pastor, the Church has decreased the number of parishes where pastoral care is entrusted to a deacon or lay person (Canon 517.2) from 447 in 2000 to 388 now (-13%). Essentially, in many dioceses, parishes are being closed rather than having these entrusted to a deacon or lay person.[148]

It is also worth noticing that the Catholic population of the United States is aging, and the new generations exhibit a much lower interest in religious affiliation. For example, 36% of young Millennials (born between 1981-1996) who presently represent the 18- 24 years of age cohort are unaffiliated with any organized religion. Additionally, 34% of older Millennials who are in the age group 25-33 also have no religious affiliation. According to the same study by the Pew Research Center the number of Christians in the US continues to decline while the number of the "nones" (those without any religious affiliation) is on the rise.

> One of the most important factors in the declining share of Christians and the growth of the "nones" is generational replacement. As the Millennial generation enters adulthood, its members display much lower levels of religious affiliation, including less connection with Christian churches, than

---

[148] Center for Applied Research in the Apostolate, Nineteen Sixty-four Blog: *Checkup Time,* (July 8, 2014), http://nineteensixty-four.blogspot.com/2014/07/checkup-time.html (accessed January 19, 2016).

older generations. Fully 36% of young Millennials (those between the ages of 18 and 24) are religiously unaffiliated as are 34% of older Millennials (ages 25-33). And fewer than six-in-ten Millennials identify with any branch of Christianity, compared with seven-in-ten or more among older generations, including Baby Boomers and Gen-Xers. Just 16% of Millennials are Catholic, and only 11% identify with mainline Protestantism. Roughly one-in-five are evangelical Protestants.[149]

The above-mentioned statistics seem to indicate that Catholic parishes will continue to decline in numbers especially in the Northeast and Midwest parts of the United States affected most by significant demographic changes in the Catholic population. Therefore, it is of grave importance to find out who has the authority to close, merge or change parish structures. In accordance with canon 515, §2, the diocesan bishop is the competent authority "to erect, suppress or alter parishes." However, the same canon states very clearly that before the bishop makes his final decision, he is to hear the presbyteral council. In recent years, the Vatican has rejected several petitions requesting the suppression of Catholic parishes in the US mainly because some bishops did not fulfill this specific requirement of the law. In addition to the presbyteral council, the bishop may also consult other individuals, consultative bodies and diocesan councils (the vicar general, vicars forane, the board of consultors, and the diocesan finance council).

Ultimately the diocesan bishop has the authority to alter, suppress and erect parishes that fall under his canonical jurisdiction. While conducting this course of action, it is advisable for the bishop to follow canon 127 which describes the process of obtaining consent and counsel. While seeking the advice of the presbyteral council, the bishop ought to create an opportunity for the members of the council to speak freely before he makes his final decision. If consent or consultation is required by law and the superior or the bishop fails to obtain it, the act (decision and decree) of such ecclesiastic authority is invalid in accordance with canon 127, §1, 2°. Such an act of the bishop would also stand in violation of canon 515, §2.

In accordance with the canonical provisions described in canons 122-123, while closing a parish or making changes to its present structure, the bishop must respect the intentions of the founders, donors, parish statutes and those who legitimately can claim parish rights. While it is impossible to obtain input from all founders and donors, it is of great importance to search the parish and the diocesan archives for relevant documents indicating the intentions of donors and founders. In cases where closures and mergers are met with strong opposition, the bishop may consider asking those who disagree with this particular course of action to provide an alternative plan within a reasonable period of time. Moreover, it is also important to

---

[149] Pew Research Center, *America's Changing Religious Landscape: Christians Decline Sharply as Share of Population; Unaffiliated and Other Faiths Continue to Grow*, (May 12, 2015), 7, Washington, D.C., http://www.pewforum.org/2015/05/12/americas-changing-religious-landscape/ (accessed January 1, 2016).

keep in mind that while the people of God have the right to pastoral care (canons 213-214), in the case of Catholic parishes it is up to the diocesan bishop to determine how this requirement can be fulfilled in their particular diocese and parish circumstances. The bishop is not required by Canon Law to obtain the consent of parishioners while considering structural changes, mergers, and closures of parishes. The bishop has the final say in such matters according to canon 515, §2. Once the bishop has obtained the input of the presbyteral council as well as the founders and the donors, he has to make the final decision. After reaching his decision, the bishop needs to issue a decree of parish suppression, merger or alteration. Such a decree must be notarized by the chancellor of the diocese. Many canon lawyers underline the importance of recording in writing different phases of the entire process by providing the minutes from the conducted meetings with dates, times and the nature of such consultation.

Some dioceses in the United States (Cleveland[150], Milwaukee[151], Philadelphia[152], Madison[153]), have developed detailed manuals and pastoral plans of assistance for pastors, parish administrators and lay leaders who may be entrusted with the responsibility to oversee mergers, closures or alteration of parish structures. Overseers involved in such cases must make sure that the real needs of parishioners and their involvement in this process take place from the very early stages until its accomplishment. Many pastoral plans underline the importance of forming the Merger/Transition Team, which is absolutely essential for such transitions to be effective. Furthermore, for the sake of justice and fairness all parishes involved in such a process should be represented by their pastors and respective parishioners, so that all people can feel that their voice is heard and well represented.

There are several different case scenarios when it comes to the closing, merging or altering parish structures. For example, two or more parishes may be asked to merge in one parish community. While implementing the merger process, the bishop may decide to sell parts of their existing parish property and to turn the church buildings into secular use. The bishop may also decide to sell all church buildings and parish properties and to build a new church in a different location that best meets the needs of the parishioners. There is always a possibility of turning some of the church buildings into chapels or oratories. The commonly used principle in such cases is that the temporal goods including parish property follow the people (canons 121 and 122). When relegating church buildings to profane use, the bishop is

---

[150] Diocese of Cleveland, OH, *Suggested Process for Merging a Parish,* (March 2009), Cleveland, OH, http://www.dioceseofcleveland.org/reconfiguration/manual/28.pdf (accessed September 21, 2016).
[151] Archdiocese of Milwaukee , *Parish Merger Process,* (2007), Milwaukee, http://www.archmil.org/Resources/Parish-Merger-Checklists.htm (accessed September 21, 2016).
[152] Archdiocese of Philadelphia, *Building a New Parish Community,* (Fall 2011), Philadelphia, http://archphila.org/conversion/bulletin/BookletIndepthEvalofParishLife.pdf (accessed September 21, 2016).
[153] Diocese of Madison, WI, *Trusting in the Spirit,* (March 2005), Madison, WI, http://www.madisondiocese.org/DioceseofMadison/Planning/TrustingintheSpirit.aspx (accessed September 21, 2016).

to hear the presbyteral council and the consent of those who are authorized to claim parish rights (canons 1214 and 1222). On May 15, 2013, the General Secretary of the United States Conference of Catholic Bishops[154] circulated a copy of a letter issued by Cardinal Mauro Piacenza. Cardinal Piacenza, the Prefect of the Congregation for the Clergy, provided a detailed explanation in regards to the Procedural Guidelines for the Modification of Parishes, the Closure or Relegation of Churches to Profane but not Sordid Use and the Alienation of the Same.[155] Any bishop or ecclesiastical superior who may consider introducing structural changes to Catholic parishes in their canonical jurisdiction ought to become familiar with this document in order to make sure that everything that they are proposing is in accordance with the norms and the practice of Church law.

---

[154] See Appendix A for the Memorandum from Msgr. Ronny E. Jenkins, General Secretary.

[155] See Appendix B for the Letter from the Congregation for the Clergy Issued by Cardinal Mauro Piacenza.

CHAPTER III.

INTRODUCTION OF THE CASE STUDY BASED ON THE DIOCESE OF YOUNGSTOWN AND DESCRIPTION OF THE BOOK METHODOLOGY

The Case of the Diocese of Youngstown

History and Background Leading to Mergers and Closures

The Catholic Diocese of Youngstown was erected by Pope Pius XII on June 4, 1943, during the turbulent times of WWII. The first bishop of the Youngstown Diocese was the Most Reverend James A. McFadden. His installation took place at St. Columba Cathedral in Youngstown, Ohio on July 22, 1943. The establishment of the new diocese was motivated by a tremendous growth of the Catholic faithful in Northeast Ohio. The Cleveland Diocese was the mother diocese that initially gave a generous portion of its geographical territory so that the Diocese of Youngstown could be established.

The Youngstown Diocese is predominantly a blue-collar diocese that stretches over six counties: Mahoning, Portage, Trumbull, Stark, Columbiana, and Ashtabula. With the collapse of the steel mill industry in 1970 which employed a vast majority of workers in the Mahoning Valley, Youngstown experienced a tremendous decline in its population. The Diocese of Youngstown had one hundred and thirteen Catholic parishes and one hundred and ten active priests when its Parish Reconfiguration Plan was released on May 28, 2010.[156] The proposed plan envisioned a twenty-five percent reduction in the number of parishes from one hundred and thirteen to eighty-seven. Bishop George V. Murry, the diocesan bishop, stated the following three reasons for the parish mergers and closure: the demographics changes affecting the number of Catholics in Youngstown, the declining number of available priests and the changing expectations of Catholic people living in the area.

The Parish Reconfiguration Plan was developed over a period of eighteen months before its final release. In the fall of 2008, all existing parishes and two missions received a self-evaluation document aimed at developing a situational audit for each parish community. The data gathered from the situational audit identified current trends in various parishes in regards to social outreach and evangelization, Mass attendance, the size of the parish community, fiscal stability as well as the demographic changes affecting the Catholic population and the overall parish vitality.

In June of 2009, the newly formed Executive Committee for Parish Planning[157] studied and evaluated all pertaining data and information collected from

---

[156] See Appendix C for the Diocese of Youngstown Reconfiguration Plan.
[157] See Appendix D for the Names of the Members of the Committee.

every parish in light of its strengths and weaknesses influencing their existing programs and services, parish vision for the future and the external threats to the parish life and ministries. Furthermore, the same committee made a recommendation in regards to parishes that should be merged, clustered or closed and those parishes that should continue their existence as a single unit. In July of 2009 parish teams were presented at various deanery meetings with the recommendations of the Executive Committee and asked for their input and comments. During those meetings diocesan officials presented various definitions and terminology used for the process of developing a reconfiguration plan.[158] Moreover, a time table on parish planning was provided for all parties involved.[159] The recommendations of the Executive Committee were made in light of the three major reasons for parish reconfiguration. The information and input obtained from parish teams were presented and discussed with each of the six deans functioning in the Diocese of Youngstown. Moreover, the deans discussed the outcome of these discussions with the priests belonging to each respective deanery. In the fall of 2009 various deanery meetings were held again in order to develop a clear plan of action for each deanery. Representatives of the Executive Committee and deans outlined individual recommendations for each of the six diocesan deaneries that have been represented by both lay and ordained people. After all the meetings were concluded the Executive Committee made their final recommendation to Bishop Murry. On February 23, 2010, a proposed draft of the reconfiguration plan was presented to pastors and parish teams. Parishes that wanted to pursue a different plan of action were asked to make their case known to Bishop Murry by March 15, 2010, and before the final promulgation of the plan. As a result, of this option, four parishes asked to continue their existence as they were and five parishes chose to enter into collaboration instead of pursuing a merger. With these adjustments in mind, the Diocese of Youngstown promulgated its official Parish Reconfiguration Plan on May 28, 2010.

General Characteristics and History of the Nine Parishes Used in this Case Study

The case study for this book reflects nine different parishes from the Diocese of Youngstown. These nine parishes have been grouped into three various sets of parishes reflecting the 2010 diocesan plan of reconfiguration. The nine parishes used in this case study have been selected because of their unique merger and closure situations as well as their ethnic diversity. The book's aim was to develop pastoral recommendations based on a rich variety of challenges affecting parishes that were asked to merge, close or to enter into a collaboration model. In addition, the three sets of parishes used for this case study represent three different cities located in the Diocese of Youngstown: Newton Falls, Warren, and Campbell. The author of this book decided to present these three sets of parishes based on the complexity of their

---

[158] See Appendix E for the Terminology Used During the Deanery Meetings.

[159] See Appendix F for the Time Table on Parish Planning.

merger, closure or collaboration situation and their ethnic diversity. In case of the city of Newton Falls, two parishes merged into one and the newly created parish unit retained all buildings and grounds. In the city of Warren, three parishes merged into one new parish unit. The new parish kept the church and social hall buildings from the former St. Joseph Church because they were in the best physical and architectural conditions. The property and church buildings of the former Christ Our King Parish and St. Pius X Parish have been sold. After the existing debt of the three parishes had been paid using the assets from the sales of their property, the remaining funds went towards the newly created parish unit. The city of Campbell presents the most complex situation regarding parish mergers, closures, and collaboration in the Diocese of Youngstown, OH.

Before the 2010 Diocesan Plan for Parish Reconfiguration was announced there were five separate parishes in the city of Campbell: St. Elizabeth Slovak Parish, St. John the Baptist Slovak Parish, St. Joseph the Provider Polish Parish, St. Lucy Italian Parish and St. Rosa de Lima Hispanic Parish. St. Elizabeth Parish was officially closed on January 2, 2011, due to declining membership and an inability to preserve vibrancy and fiscal stability. The remaining four parishes in the city of Campbell entered into a merger and collaboration model based on the service of one pastor, one associate pastor, two worship sites and a creation of a Pastoral Team.

For the purpose of this study it is important to present a clear understanding of terminology used by the Diocese of Youngstown in reference to various parish structural changes. A clustered parish was understood as a grouping of two or more parishes served by one or more priests. The parishes belonging to a cluster retained separate church and parish buildings as well as their separate identities (finance and parish councils, day to day operations and administration). Cluster parishes have been encouraged to share their resources, programs, and ministries. A merged parish was understood as a joining of two or more parishes in order to create a new single parish unit or consolidated parish. In this case there is one parish and finance council, one parish staff and one canonically erected new parish unit. In the merger model there can be single or multiple worship sites depending on individual cases and circumstances of the parishes involved in this process.

The City of Newton Falls and the Merger of St. Mary Polish Parish with St. Joseph Slovak Parish.

The first set of parishes used for this case study comes from the small city of Newton Falls, Ohio, where there were two Catholic parishes in existence separated by less than half a mile geographical distance. One of those parishes was St. Mary Polish Parish, initially founded as a parish mission by Polish immigrants and their descendants in 1927. This parish was erected as a national and not a territorial parish. The canonical status of St. Mary's Parish was changed in 1964 from being a national parish to a territorial parish. In 1928 St. Mary became a fully-fledged parish recognized by the Diocese of Youngstown under the name of Our Lady of Czestochowa (Matka Boska Czestochowska). However, most parishioners and Newton Falls residents continued to refer to the Polish Parish as St. Mary's Church.

Across the river on the other side of town, the Slovak community established a Catholic mission on January 21, 1923. A month later, on February 27, 1923, the mission became a canonical parish under the patronage of St. Joseph. The first church building was dedicated on December 24, 1923. Both parishes continued their separate existence until 1994. From July of 1994 until May 2008 both parishes began to share one pastor who ministered to their spiritual needs. This change was affected by the ongoing shortage of available priests in the diocese. Supporting two competing Catholic churches in a small city of Newton Falls proved to be an ongoing struggle and challenge. As early as 1971 both parishes were asked by Bishop Malone to consider merging into one unified parish community. Unfortunately, a fierce opposition and strong emotions expressed by members of both parishes prevented any structural changes until 2008. Since 1970 when the Youngstown Steel Mills began to shut down its operations, the number of parishioners at both respective churches began to decline. In July of 2006 when the author of this book became the newly appointed pastor of both parishes, St. Mary had fewer than a hundred registered members. Registrations at St. Joseph Parish were slightly above three hundred families at that time.

With the appointment of a new pastor, an Ad Hoc Committee represented by active members from both parishes was established. The committee spent quality time discussing the present needs and challenges affecting both parishes. Additionally, members of the committee helped to develop a parish-wide survey which was presented to all interested parties in order to hear the voice of the people in the pews. After the results of the survey had been analyzed and presented to all parishioners, the Ad Hoc Committee made a unanimous recommendation to merge both parishes into one single parish unit with one pastor, one worship site and one parish and finance council.[160] The reasons for the merger were the declining number of the Catholic population in the area as well as the lack of financial stability at St. Mary Parish and the overall lack of vibrancy at both parishes. Combining people and available resources in order to create a new parish unit seemed to be the best logical and pastoral option at that time. With the appointment of the new bishop, in 2007, when the Most Reverend George V. Murry, S.J., became the ordinary of the Youngstown Diocese the Consolidation Plan for St. Mary and St. Joseph parishes was accepted.[161] A decree of merger was issued by Bishop George V. Murry on May 13, 2008.[162] The newly formed parish unit was named as St. Mary and St. Joseph Parish in order to preserve the tradition and the history of both merging parishes. The Newton Falls merger was one of the most successful mergers in the Diocese of Youngstown at that time. Furthermore, it is also important to remember that this merger took place two years before the diocesan-wide reconfiguration plan had been announced.

---

[160] See Appendix G for the Newton Falls Consolidation Plan and Survey Results.

[161] See Appendix H for the Letter of Acceptance of Plan by Bishop Murry.

[162] See Appendix I for the Decree of Merger.

The City of Warren and the Merger of Christ Our King, St. Pius X and St. Joseph Polish Parish.

The second set of parishes used for this case study represents three parishes from the city of Warren, Ohio. Although all three parishes involved in this merger (St. Joseph Polish Parish, Christ Our King and St. Pius X Parish) were located on the west side of Warren, all three of them had different origins and ethnic make-up. St. Joseph Polish Parish was established on July 6, 1928, by a group of descendants of Polish immigrants who came to the Youngstown area at the end of the 19th century. St. Joseph's parishioners built their church themselves using the scarce financial and building resources available to them during the time of the Great Depression. The first church building was dedicated on October 13, 1929, by Bishop Joseph Schrembs of the Cleveland Diocese. A very touching mention of this event had been written in the book entitled; The March of the Eucharist.[163] This inspiring timepiece was published by the Diocese of Youngstown in 1951, eight years after the newly erected diocese was established. The book contains the history of all Youngstown parishes that were in existence at that time. In 1964, a new church building was built and dedicated by Bishop Emmett Walsh. St. Joseph Parish continued to grow in size and numbers until the early 1980s. With the passing of time St. Joseph Parish experienced a gradual decline in the number of parish families, Mass attendance and parish ministries and services. In 2010 when the Diocese of Youngstown announced the reconfiguration plan, St. Joseph Parish was asked to merge with Pius X Parish and Christ Our King Parish. These three church communities created a new single parish unit in 2011 under the patronage of St. John Paul II. Initially, the newly appointed pastor Rev. H celebrated masses and the sacraments at three different worship sites. Presently, the property and the church building of the former St. Joseph Parish serves as a worship site for the newly established parish. The properties and church buildings from the other two parishes were sold and designated for profane usage.

St. Pius X Parish was established on July 3, 1959, by Bishop Emmett M. Walsh of the Youngstown Diocese. The church and the school buildings were completed in 1961. The first mass at St. Pius X Church was celebrated on August 6, 1961. St. Pius X Parish was a true Catholic American melting pot of many diverse cultures, traditions and nationalities. People of Irish, German, Italian and all-American origins came together to establish this unique parish community. The parish had a vibrant school and many ministries serving the needs of the Catholics who lived in the area. St. Pius X parish community continued to grow in size and numbers until early 1990. From that point onwards St. Pius X Parish, just like many other parishes in the Youngstown Diocese at that time, experienced a serious decline in the number of active parishioners. With the closing of the parish school and the demographic changes affecting the Catholic population in the city of Warren, St. Pius X Parish entered into a merger process with Christ Our King Parish and St. Joseph Polish Parish in 2010.

---

[163] *The March of the Eucharist*, (Youngstown: Diocese of Youngstown, 1951), 211.

Inspired by the growth of the Catholic population in the city of Warren after WWII, Christ Our King Parish was erected in September of 1951. The parish church, just like that of St. Pius X church was a combination of a church and school building. The sanctuary area of the church looked more like an auditorium than anything else. The parishioners of Christ Our King Parish built not only the church but also a school (1953) and a convent building. It is estimated that approximately 1000 families belonged to Christ our King Parish at the peak of its popularity. People of different nationalities and place of origin claimed Christ Our King Parish to be their spiritual home. In June of 1972 due to an insufficient number of students and the high cost of education, Christ Our King Catholic School closed its doors. By 1993, the number of parish families was reduced to three hundred and forty. The 2010 Diocese of Youngstown Parish Reconfiguration Plan recommended that Christ Our King Parish to merge with St. Joseph Polish Parish and St. Pius X Parish. All of these parishes were located in the City of Warren on the west side.

The City of Campbell and the Merger, Closure and Collaboration of St. John the Baptist Slovak Parish, St. Joseph the Provider Polish Parish, St. Lucy Italian Parish and St. Rosa de Lima Hispanic Parish.

The third and the most culturally and ethnically diverse set of parishes used for this case study came from the city of Campbell, Ohio. The city of Campbell was called for a long time "the city of churches." While the diocesan plan of reconfiguration was announced in May of 2010, the actual merging, closing and collaborating of parishes did not take place in most cases until June of 2011 when twenty-six priests received their new assignments and recommendations to implement parish structural changes. In regards to the city of Campbell, four ethnically and culturally diverse Catholic parishes, St. John the Baptist Slovak Parish, St. Joseph the Provider Polish Parish (formerly known as St. John the Baptist Polish Parish), St. Lucy Italian-American Parish and Santa Rosa de Lima Hispanic Parish, entered into a merger/closure/collaboration process. St. Lucy and Santa Rosa de Lima Parishes merged in 2010. Initially, when the newly appointed pastor and the associate pastor began their ministry in the city of Campbell in 2011, the two of them had to cover three different worship sites. Eighteen months later the pastor was re-assigned to a different parish community, and the associate pastor became the proper pastor of the newly formed parish unit called Christ Our Shepherd Parish. In February 2015, the Diocese of Youngstown announced the closure of St. Lucy and Santa Rosa de Lima Hispanic Parish. The daily Masses were to be held at St. John the Baptist Slovak Church and the weekend, feast day and holiday Masses were to be held at St. Joseph the Provider Polish Church. Merging four culturally and ethnically diverse Catholic parishes into a single parish unit with two worship sites proved to be one of the most challenging cases envisioned by the 2010 Diocese of Youngstown Parish Reconfiguration Plan. Strong opinions and feelings expressed by Campbell's cohort in the survey presented by the author of this book show how painful and difficult parish mergers can be in real life situations. The Campbell parishes have been working on the actual merger for the last five years, and it still seems that many people are very dissatisfied with the final outcome of the parish reconfiguration plan.

One of the parishes involved in this merger situation was St. John the Baptist Slovak Parish. The Slovak settlers who came to the Mahoning Valley in search of work at Youngstown steel mill established St. John the Baptist Slovak Parish in September of 1919. The existing church was built in 1954. The parish had its own school, cemetery, convent and a social hall. In the last two decades, the number of active parish members and financial supporters who helped the parish to stay afloat declined dramatically. As a result, of demographic changes and membership decline St. John the Baptist Parish was recommended by the diocesan plan to merge with St. Joseph the Provider Polish Parish, St. Lucy Italian-American Parish and Santa Rosa de Lima Hispanic Parish.

St. Joseph the Provider Polish Parish, was initially erected in 1919 by Polish immigrants as St. John the Baptist Polish Parish. The first church building was dedicated on August 19, 1920. As the parish continued to grow a new rectory, school and convent were built in 1963. The Most Reverend Emmett M. Walsh, the second bishop of Youngstown granted his permission in1961 for the new church to be erected under the patronage of St. Joseph the Provider. When the Youngstown steel mill industry begun to suffer in the early1970s, St. Joseph Parish lost a lot of parish members who moved out of the area in search of available employment. The condition and structure of the existing St. Joseph the Provider church building and well-maintained parish grounds became the selling point in the process of choosing a worship site for the newly formed parish unit under the name of Christ the Good Shepherd Parish.

St. Lucy Catholic Parish was erected on June 18, 1937, by Bishop Schrembs from the Cleveland Diocese at the request of the Italian Catholic Society. Italian immigrants came to the city of Campbell, Ohio in early 1900 to seek employment at the Republic Iron and Steel Company in Youngstown, Ohio. Their persistence to protect, continue and cultivate their Italian-American heritage inspired the formation of a new church under the patronage of St. Lucy. Bishop James A. McFadden, the first bishop of the Youngstown Diocese dedicated the church on October 26, 1952. Pope Pius XII established the Catholic Diocese of Youngstown on June 4, 1943, due to a growing number of Catholics in Northeast Ohio. With the passing of time St. Lucy Parish became the American melting pot of different cultures, traditions and nationalities. From the late 1990s St. Lucy Parish experienced the sad reality of declining membership numbers and the overall trends affecting the demographics of the Catholic population in Northeast Ohio. As a result, St. Lucy merged with Santa Rosa de Lima Hispanic Parish in 2010.

The Parish of Santa Rosa de Lima St. Rose of Lima has a rich and turbulent history. It seems that the Hispanic people who came to the area have constantly been on the move as far as their spiritual home was concerned. Hispanic immigrants came to the Mahoning Valley as early as the 1920s and the 1930s. As the Youngstown steel industry continued to expand, reliable workforce was needed and desperately wanted. A large number of Hispanics immigrated to the Mahoning Valley from Puerto Rico especially in 1942 and 1960. Since Puerto Rico became an American territory due to the Spanish-American War of 1898, it was much easier for the people of Puerto Rico to travel to the mainland USA. Searching for good paying jobs and new opportunities to better their families and themselves, many Puerto Rican families migrated to Youngstown in order to start their new lives. They were hard working people with exemplary work ethics.

As the Hispanic population continued to grow in size and since the majority of them were Catholic, they wanted to have their own Catholic parish. With the help of Bishop James McFadden of the Youngstown Diocese, a new Spanish-speaking parish was established in 1953. Prior to this establishment, the Spanish-speaking people worshiped in the old church of St. John the Baptist in Campbell as well as in the basement of St. Columba Cathedral. Initially, the newly erected parish took ownership of an Italian Protestant church located on Himrod Street. However, a few years later the church property was acquired by the US government and the Spanish speaking people had to search for yet another location for their church. Finally, in January of 1961, they moved to a different location on Struthers-Coitsville Road where they realized their longed hoped for dream of having a permanent residence in the Youngstown Diocese. Since 1970, the Parish of St. Rose of Lima had been ministered to by the Spanish speaking Missionaries of the Precious Blood, who came to the Mahoning Valley to work specifically with the Hispanic immigrants. On November 19, 2005 the Hispanic community had to move to yet another location due to the deteriorating condition of their church building. They found their home together with the congregation of St. Lucy's Catholic Parish where they continued their worship until the Diocese of Youngstown announced its Parish Plan of Reconfiguration in 2010.

Research Methodology

The aim of this book was to research and examine a wide variety of Catholic parishioners who participated in the process of merging, closing and collaborating of parishes in order to develop helpful pastoral recommendations. The research methodology was a combination of qualitative and quantitative research methods. The questions used in the survey were formulated in order to gain a better understanding of participants' motivations and driving forces behind their opinions and emotions. It was essential for the integrity of this research to quantify the data especially in regards to participants' attitudes and convictions in regards to parish structural changes and alterations. The interviews and conversations with the pastors involved in the process of merging, closing and collaborating of parishes had proven to be a vital source of information.

The intention of the author of this book was to measure the level of respondent participation in the process of developing and implementing a pastoral plan for parishes as well as the participants' feelings about the ongoing communication, people's expectations, and opinions regarding the process. Parishioners who experienced first-hand the undeniable reality of parish closures and mergers need a forum to share their feelings and opinions. Additionally, they need to develop healthy ways of dealing with an ongoing change and transformation of parish structures which affect their lives. It was a sincere hope of the author of this book to create such a forum and to allow the respondents to be brutally honest about their points of view, hurts, and struggles as well as positive outcomes which accompany the process of structural changes affecting Catholic parishes.

The three pastors involved in this study were instrumental in sharing and providing their opinions, accomplishments and hardships especially during the implementation phase of the process. All three pastors were asked to provide at least ten names of parishioners from each of their respective parishes involved in a merger, closure or collaboration, who would be interested and willing to participate in the survey by sharing their insights and opinions. As a result, the three pastors pointed out the names of parishioners who have been a part of the process of merging, closing, and collaboration. Many of the survey respondents have been lifetime parish members while others joined their respective parish communities within the last decade. The sampling of participants has been very diverse regarding their ethnic background, age, gender, level of education and participation in the life of their parishes. One of the common factors for all of the respondents was their level of honesty. It was a humbling experience for the author of this book to read all surveys and to immerse himself once again in the challenges associated with the parish structural changes and alterations. Sometimes the pain and grief expressed by the respondents was overwhelming. At other times their understanding of what it means to be a parish community and what it means to be a member of that parish community was very touching and inspiring.

Survey Development and Rationale

Following the Lincoln and Guba "maximum variation sampling,"[164] the author of this book decided to administer the survey to a wide variety of respondents recommended by their respective pastors. Choosing nine culturally, historically and ethnically diverse parish communities guaranteed a rich sampling of people involved in the process of merging, closing and collaborating of parishes. Parishioners affected by the process had much to say about it, and they were very forthcoming and honest about it. The author of this book designed the format of the survey in such a way as to present people's feelings and opinions about the process. In addition, the intent of the survey was to make comparisons between different parishes and to demonstrate the level of parishioners' understanding of what worked well and what could have been done better as they were going through parish structural changes. Honesty and transparency were the key themes behind the design of the survey. The sampling of the lived experience of the survey participants had proven to be very rich and diverse in providing the complexity of the problem. In addition, Tim Sensing's samples of the Consent Form for Interview and a Questionnaire had been used for this book as guiding principles for the development of the survey.[165]

---

[164] Tim Sensing, *Qualitative Research, A Multi-Method Approach to Books for Doctor of Ministry Theses* (Eugine, OR: Wipf and Stock Publishers, 2011), 84.

Survey Questions, a Coding System, Timeline, and Mailings

The parish communities represented in this research consisted of two parishes in Newton Falls that have been merged into one parish, three parishes in Warren that have been merged into one parish, and four parishes in Campbell that have been engaged in a process of collaboration and merger for several years. Some survey questions were formulated with respect to measuring the attitudes of parishioners who were involved in parish life during the process of merger, collaboration or closing. Some questions were formulated as open-ended questions. Other questions and especially question number seven were quite elaborate. Question number seven was based on a rating scale from 1 – meaning Strongly Agree to 5 – meaning Strongly Disagree. In addition to several demographic questions, there were other important questions developed for each of the following areas:

I. Was there organizational, communication, implementation and assessment support provided by the diocese?
II. How were parishioners and the parish community involved in the process?
III. Did parishioners feel informed and did they feel their feelings were considered in the process?
IV. Was there consideration given as to the impact this process would have on parishioners and the parish community? Were there positive outcomes?
V. What consideration and support was given to the pastors in terms of preparation, guidance, and access to consultants and support.
VI. What worked well? What didn't work well? How could this process be improved.

A coding system was developed to help track all responses. Each respondent was assigned a unique four-digit access code.
With the four digit access code, the first digit
stands for the number of parishes in that
area - 4 for Campbell, 3 for Warren and 2 for
Newton Falls. The second digit refers to the parish number 1-4 in Campbell, 1-3 in Warren and 1-2 in Newton Falls. The last two digits represent parishioner numbers 01 thru 15.

---

[165] Tim Sensing, *Qualitative Research, A Multi-Method Approach to Books for Doctor of Ministry Theses* (Eugine, OR: Wipf and Stock Publishers, 2011), 235-236 and 239-241.

Table 1. Parishioner Access Codes

Parish	Parishioner Access Codes	Pastor code
Campbell St John the Baptist	4101 thru 4115	4000
Campbell St Joseph the Provider	4201 thru 4215	
Campbell St Lucy	4301 thru 4315	
Campbell St Rosa de Lima	4401 thru 4415	
Warren Christ Our King	3101 thru 3115	3000
Warren St Joseph	3201 thru 3215	
Warren St Pius X	3301 thru 3315	
Newton Falls St Joseph	2101 thru 2115	2000
Newton Falls St Mary	2201 thru 2215	

A full copy of the survey with all questions used for this reasearch is located in Appendix J. Current pastors of the parishes involved in the study were asked to identify at least ten parishioners from each of the parishes in their communities and submit those names to receive a mailing of the survey and instructions for return.[166] The pastors were asked on May 19, 2015 to identify potential survey participants by June 4, 2015. Once the names of potential participants were received, surveys were mailed on June 18, 2015 with instructions to return an attached postcard indicating a willingness to complete the survey as well as the instructions for completing the survey and mailing it back, or completing it online.[167] The participants were asked to complete their surveys by July 4, 2015. For some participants, the deadline to complete the survey was extended considering the fact that the mailing took place during summer vacation. A follow up letter was mailed on July 17, 2015[168] and a thank you letter was mailed on August 6, 2015.[169]

The author of this book received a total of 88 surveys returned out of 111 mailed. The high number of respondents was a powerful indication about parishioners' feelings and opinions regarding the subject at hand. The vast majority of survey respondents welcomed an opportunity to speak about the process of developing and implementing of the pastoral plan. Many respondents completed their survey online. All paper surveys returned to the author of this book were hand entered into the online interface so that results could be compiled and create an easily accessible data. As mentioned before, the scaling data for Question seven ranged

---

[166] See Appendix K Sample Letter to the Pastor.

[167] See Appendix L Cover Letter and Post Card to Prospective Parishioner Respondents.

[168] See Appendix M for the Follow Up Letter.

[169] See Appendix N for the Thank You Letter.

from 1 – Strongly Agree to 5 – Strongly Disagree. A thorough examination of the data regarding Question seven yields results that are very different for each of the three sets of parish communities involved. Complete survey data can be viewed in Appendix O.

It is important to note that the length of time that has passed since the merger, closure/collaboration began is significantly different between the three sets of parish communities. When the survey was administered in the summer of 2015, the parishes in Newton Falls have been merged for almost 7 years and they seemed to feel positive about their experience and the overall results. The Warren parishes have been involved in the process of merging for 4 years at that time, and they were beginning to express more positive feelings about the process. However, the parishes in Campbell have discussed and participated in the process since 2010 but not until 2015 have they been faced with the reality of closing of their parishes and churches. The overall results received from the four parishes in Campbell, as seen in the data, show less acceptance of the process and many negative emotions expressed by the survey respondents. The lesson to be learned from the Campbell parishes is to make sure that the process is not only well explained but that it is also well executed in a timely manner. In other words, the process of implementation should not be too hasty nor should it be too slow.

CHAPTER IV.

SUMMARY AND ANALYSIS OF DATA

General Analysis

The general overview of collected data from the nine parishes who participated in this case study proves that all respondents were painfully honest and quite expressive while sharing their feelings and emotions. Although a great number of participants was convinced about the undeniable necessity of a merger, closure or collaboration, many had hoped that their church would continue to function as the main worship site. When this expectation was not met, anger, resentment, a sense of betrayal and hurt feelings followed. The people involved in this study were mostly represented by women rather than men. A significant number of respondents have been parish members for a period between twenty-five and fifty years. In Campbell, twenty-eight percent of respondents were older than seventy-five. The age of the majority of respondents was between fifty-five and over seventy-five. The level of education is widely represented from high school graduates all the way to the recipients of a graduate degree. In regards to ethnic diversity, the city of Campbell emerged as the most diverse Catholic population used in this study.

Surprising Results

It was surprising to see that parishioners from Newton Falls expressed happiness and contentment with the implementation, reasoning and the overall outcomes of the merger process which took place in 2008. The author of this book is convinced that the time factor (seven years since the merger took place) as well as the early initiative to merge before the Diocesan Parish Plan for Reconfiguration was put into place in 2010 became fundamental elements contributing to a successful accomplishment of the merger. Time indeed heals some wounds even those inflicted several decades ago. The Warren parishes are slowly coming together as one although the diehard former St. Joseph parishioners continue to be resilient to any change regardless of the logic behind it. A good number of participants felt that the diocese lacked quality communication, transparency, ongoing support and clear directions for the implementation of the plan of reconfiguration. The lack of specific timelines, goals, and objectives reflecting the plan were the biggest downfall according to some survey participants. Some respondents and especially the Catholic faithful from Campbell became very disenchanted if not plain angry with the Bishop and the diocesan officials. Many parishioners from Campbell felt that the implementation of the process took too long and it had been done poorly. Others felt that combining four very different ethnically and culturally Catholic parishes under the guidance of young priests may not have been the greatest of ideas. A great number of respondents felt that the decision had already been made from the top down and that their input and opinion was not valued. A great number of parishioners from Newton Falls and Warren tend to agree that the merger was successful and made their new parish community stronger. In contrast, more than half of the respondents from Campbell were in opposition to this statement.

Common Trends and Observations

The prevailing opinion among most survey participants in regards to the role their pastors played in the process of merging and closing and their ability to share and explain pertaining information was positive. Many respondents expressed their empathy and support for parish leaders who were tasked to oversee the implementation of the process. The vast majority of people who participated in this study emphasized the great need for formal and ritual opportunities to mourn and grieve their loss. It seems that this part of the process needs more attention and development in order to serve the needs of all parishioners who are in transition. All respondents agreed that the implementation of the process had been difficult and challenging. Many respondents were unsure whether the diocese gave adequate consideration regarding the health of the priests who were asked to implement the plan. The same was implied in regards to the pastors' training and available consultation and support while executing the plan of reconfiguration. Furthermore, none of the nine selected parish communities felt that the diocese provided a clear sense of direction and a manageable timeline for the implementation of the plan. Almost fifty percent of all respondents were unsure, whether or not the diocese has assessed the impact the process of merging, closing and collaborating would have on their parish communities. The ongoing communication between the respective parishes and the diocese had been described by many as lacking or nonexistent.

Additional Analysis

Survey respondents were asked to be honest, and all of them had fulfilled this request exceeding my greatest expectations. I was very touched and humbled that out of one hundred and eleven surveys sent out I received eighty-eight responses. The survey return rate of 79% was a great indication of how important the subject at hand is and how strongly people feel about it. Parish mergers, closures, and collaborations have a tremendous impact on entire communities and individual people's lives. It is important to remember that there was a significant time difference in the adaptation and implementation stages of the process affecting the nine parishes involved in this study. Time factor plays a significant role in both the planning and the implementation stages of the process. For example, there was a much greater acceptance and appreciation of the merger process and its impact on the Newton Falls parishes in comparison with the Warren and Campbell parishes. The Newton Falls parishioners experienced the process of merger seven years ago at the time when this study was conducted. A new parish unit was erected with one worship site and one resident pastor. What has been in the making for thirty-seven years finally came to fulfillment in 2008 when the descendants of the Polish and Slovak immigrants buried the hatchet and came together as members of St. Mary and St. Joseph Parish. What seemed to be quite impossible and improbable finally became a reality for the benefit of the entire community. All of this has been accomplished in Newton Falls two years before the diocesan-wide reconfiguration plan was announced. When the author of this book analyzed the results of the survey, he was very happily surprised to see that Newton Falls parishioners expressed the highest level of acceptance and satisfaction with the outcome of the merger.

The study and research connected with this book yielded additional surprising results. The set of the three Warren parishes which merged into one new parish unit some four years ago under the patronage of St. John Paul II, also shows more acceptance and appreciation of the merger process. Ironically, the parishioners of the former Christ Our King and St. Pius X whose churches were closed are happier with the results and the process of merger then the parishioners of the former St. Joseph Polish Parish whose church is being used as a present worship site. However, the four parishes from Campbell came across as being the least accepting of the reasons and the process of merging as envisioned by the diocesan plan of reconfiguration. One frequently mentioned observation by the Campbell parishioners was a criticism of taking too much time (over five years) to implement the mergers and the closures of Catholic parishes from that area. There is an important lesson to be learned from them, and the lesson is that parish structural changes must be implemented in a timely fashion. Although each parish merger is different from the other, prolonging the inevitable does not always work to the benefit of the process. The time factor is imperative at all stages of the process, including the planning, the development, and the implementation.

Additionally, many respondents from all nine parishes expressed a great level of dissatisfaction with the overall diocesan communication, support, and presence during the various stages of the process. Some respondents expressed their harsh feelings regarding these essential elements of the process. Many people felt that the diocese should be more visible at parish town hall meetings and other official gatherings relating to the mergers and closures of parishes. What became apparent was the importance of an ongoing communication for the success of the entire process regarding parish structural changes. The pastors involved in this study reiterated this truth over and over again in their survey responses and during our private interviews and conversations. The success of the entire process is greatly influenced and dependant upon the flow of information. Diocesan and parish communication with the parishioners ought to be frequent, edifying, consistent and presented in various forms using modern technology. One of the pastors involved in this study generated over thirty-six mailings, e-mails, bulletin inserts, etc., in the first year of parish merger. To his utmost surprise, there still were some members of his parish community who told him they have not heard a thing as to why their parish had to merge. The lesson from his experience is that parish leaders overseeing the process must never underestimate the power of communication and its frequency. Just because something had been said a hundred times it does not mean that all people are actually familiar with it. Furthermore, it is also vital to remember that sometimes people hear what they want to hear, and the message we try to deliver is not always received the same way by all who hear it. Ongoing communication and the consistency and frequency of information sharing should never be underestimated in the process of merging, closing and collaborating of parishes.

One of the most unexpected findings was the realization of the author of this book regarding parishioners' understanding of what it means to be a member of a church community. It became apparent that some people confuse being a member of a parish with being a member of an exclusive country club or some other elitist organization. The sense of a Catholic identity among some respondents is associated more so with the parish buildings and grounds and religious art effects rather than the shared values, beliefs and a sense of community created for a specific mission and vision. The development and implementation of a parish mission and vision are imperative for all Catholic parishes. If we want to create vibrant Catholic parishes with a specific purpose for their existence rooted in the mission of Jesus and a vision for the future, then we need to start with helping our parishioners to form and to assert their Catholic identity. People ought to be educated and informed about what it means to be Catholic and what it means to be a member of a Catholic church community with all rights and obligations. The formation of intentional disciples ought to be an integral part of every parish mission and vision. If Catholic parishes are to remain relevant in the lives of their respective members, they need to meet their people wherever they are presently in their lives and faith journeys. Catholic parishes ought to present the message of the Gospel anew as they promote and actively participate in the process of the New Evangelization.

A significant number of survey respondents expressed their appreciation for creating a forum to express their feelings, opinions and as well as an evaluation of the process. Many survey participants, including the author of this book, commended the Diocese of Youngstown for allowing a sufficient amount of time to develop the first draft of the reconfiguration plan based on the parish self-evaluation instrument. Much appreciation was given to the four diocesan-wide deanery meetings where both lay and ordained church members were actively involved in the process of developing the plan and formulating the reasons behind it. Some parishioners felt that additional opportunities to voice their opinions and to provide input should be provided during the planning and the implementation stages of the process. The data collected from the survey shows that the lay faithful want to be actively involved in the process from the early stages of its development until its implementation. The people in the pews want to have their voices heard and be taken seriously by parish and diocesan leaders.

Both lay and ordained participants of the survey pointed out two important elements of the diocesan reconfiguration plan that could have been done more efficiently. The first of them was the lack of a detailed, step by step implementation plan with specific timelines, deadlines and goals, and objectives. If all parties involved in the process are well informed about what they are expected to do, how to do it and when it must be done, the implementation stage of the process will become most effective. Unfortunately, that part of the Diocese of Youngstown Parish Reconfiguration Plan was non-existent. The second important element of the diocesan plan apparently missing was the development and the provision of some form of an evaluation tool for the process. Pastors, parish leaders, and parishioners need an easy to apply evaluation tool to assess the progress of the implementation process, its effectiveness, and outcomes. Evaluations are essential in order to see what worked well and what could have been done better.

While designing the format of the survey the researcher tried very hard to remain objective and not to impose any subjective responses on the survey participants. What became clear during the analysis of the survey results was that many respondents simply did not know or were unsure if they could provide an honest answer. For example, many parishioners did not know whether their pastor received sufficient and ongoing support from the diocese. Moreover, survey participants were unsure if the diocese considered the priest's health and well-being while asking him to oversee a merger, closure or collaboration process. What seemed to be a very positive aspect of the Youngstown plan was its intentional objective to merge parish congregations rather than to push for immediate closures and suppression of Catholic parishes and churches. This is not to say that all involved parties were completely satisfied with the final outcomes of the reconfiguration plan. It is simply an observation which speaks in favor of the Diocese of Youngstown approach to the subject of parish mergers, closures, and collaborations.

The pastor-researcher who designed the survey was very humbled by people's responses and honesty. The open-ended questions provided an additional and much needed insight into this research. Being a pastor of two, three or four Catholic parishes that are going through the process of structural changes is a demanding task, a great responsibility, and a far-reaching undertaking. The development and the implementation of the process affect all parties involved on many different levels, and it can evoke some strong feelings, opinions, and emotions. William Shakespeare could not have said it better in his play: *King Henry the Fourth; "Uneasy lies the head that wears a crown."* In most cases pastors and parish leaders do not get a chance to receive an honest input and evaluation from the parishioners involved in the process. Sometimes priest pastors are being re-assigned to other parish communities before they can evaluate what worked well and what could have been done better in the process. At times, it is indeed unfortunate that those who had been tasked with the implementation of the process do not get a chance to see whether their hard work and endless efforts to guide, console and shepherd the people of God and their parishes in transition had been fruitful and life-giving. This research has brought its author much needed closure and appreciation for everything that took place while overseeing a parish merger, even when at times it was difficult and emotionally draining. Because of this research, the author came to a full realization that all the hard work and challenges connected with the process helped at the end to create a strong and unified parish community. It was truly uplifting to see after several years went by how the members of the newly erected parish community in Newton Falls came to a fuller realization of what it means to be a member of a Catholic parish, especially while going through a major structural transition.

CHAPTER V.

PASTORAL REFLECTION

Recommended Pastoral Practices for Merging, Closing, and Collaborating of Parishes

The aims of this book were to provide some pastoral recommendations based on the existing pastoral plans and the book survey results for pastors, parish leaders, and parishioners who are going through the process of parish structural changes. Therefore, it seems appropriate to provide a concise list of recommended pastoral practices while considering parish mergers, closures, and collaborations. The following list of recommended pastoral practices has been developed by the author of this book from numerous resources pertaining to the subject at hand:

1. Involve and encourage lay and ordained people to be a part of the entire process and all of its different stages: planning and development, implementation and evaluation.
2. A self-evaluation of parish vibrancy is indispensable. It should take place before specific structural changes can be introduced.
3. Provide exact reasons for the change and transition and create a vision for the future. Parishioners should be informed about the expected outcomes of the process.
4. Communicate frequently, communicate efficiently and communicate some more using all available means and methods. Communicate with the parishioners, the bishop and other people involved. Shared information must be consistent at all times.
5. Provide the information requested by parishioners and the diocese in a timely and organized manner (financial data, condition of existing buildings, parking lots and needed renovations).
6. Listen to the voices of all parties involved in this process. Be transparent and promote open dialogue and the willingness to compromise. When everything is set in stone, people participating in the process may become discouraged to continue their future involvement.
7. Develop a step by step strategic plan of implementation and task various groups and committees with the pursuit of its goals and objectives, for example, communication committee, religious art affects committee, hospitality and welcome committee, parish records committee, etc.
8. Specify achievable timelines and benchmarks to keep track of the ongoing progress.
9. If you must close churches, do it gradually and provide ample opportunities for parishioners to grieve, to share their stories and to mourn their loss.
10. If possible, use available rituals for parish closings as a way of providing a forum for the public expression of grief caused by the process.
11. Create numerous opportunities for suggestions, opinions, and people's input, for example, town hall meetings, listening sessions with grief counselors, Q and A boxes, e-mails, surveys, assigned phone lines, etc.

12. Be flexible and always look at what is in the best interest of all parties involved instead of just a selected few people with hidden agendas.
13. Organize liturgies, dinners and get together events between blending parish communities.
14. Pray with and for all parties involved in the process and ask for God's help, guidance and assistance. If God is not a part of this process all of our efforts are futile.

Elements of the Process Requiring Pastoral Sensitivity and Special Attention

The following elements require additional attention and sensitivity while proposing parish structural changes:

1. Listen to your people and do not ignore their input and opinion.
2. Respect the dignity of all parishioners from the blending parish families, no matter how diverse or how different they may be.
3. Honor their past history and never ever criticize their previous pastors and parish leaders.
4. Become involved in the grieving process by providing ways and methods to express parishioners' grief and to find some healing in the midst of it all. Never underestimate the depth of their pain and sorrow.
5. Cry with them, laugh with them and help them to see that sometimes change is necessary and life-giving for the future generations.
6. Do not play favorites. All people deserve to be treated with the same respect and sensitivity.
7. Do not pretend that you know it all. Always seek help and professional advice.
8. Last but not least, it is a healthy and wise practice to assign new pastors who will oversee parish structural changes. When this happens, nobody can accuse the diocese or the pastor of being partial.

CHAPTER VI.

CONCLUSION

Lessons Learned and Further Recommendations

Looking back at the theoretical and theological groundings and the survey data, the author of this book sincerely hopes that the wider ministerial community will find this project research to be beneficial and of value for the future life of Catholic parishes. The reality is that parish mergers, closures, and collaborations will continue in the future. Hopefully, parish leaders and parishioners can find some ideas, recommendations and words of wisdom based on lived experiences as they embark on a journey aimed at parish structural changes. The recommended pastoral practices reflect a collective wisdom of pastors, parish leaders, diocesan officials and parishioners who experienced the process first hand at its various stages. While no single book can address all issues connected with the process of parish mergers, closures, and collaborations, I truly hope that this book will shed some new light on different aspects of parish structural changes. Those responsible for the development and implementation of parish reconfiguration plans ought to remember that parishioners in transition want to have their voices heard. Furthermore, they want to have their opinion valued and incorporated into the final form of the reconfiguration plan. When the final decision regarding parish mergers, closures, and collaboration is perceived by parishioners and parish leaders as a top-down decision, the acceptance of the process and the reasons behind it will become much harder to achieve. On the other hand, when the decision is perceived as a process built from the bottom up, allowing for parishioners' active involvement and input, the greater the final results and acceptance of the process will be. Lay and ordained members of the Church on parish and diocesan levels need to learn how to work together instead of working against each other.

A part of this problem is rooted in the overall understanding of the role and relationship between the diocese and a local parish. A limited understanding on the part of some Catholic faithful regarding the role and function of the diocesan bishop and the diocesan curia and their relationship with local parishes seems to be at the center of this problem. One of the recommended solutions could be a more conscientious effort to educate, explain and to provide adequate information about the role of a particular diocesan church and its relationship with local parishes and the Universal Church. It could be of great help for all parties involved in this process to deepen their knowledge about the role of local parishes and their participation in the mission of the diocesan and Universal Church.

Furthermore, a refresher course on what it means to be a member of a Catholic parish community is highly recommended for all Catholic parishes including those going through parish structural changes. All parish members should be made aware of their rights and obligations as well as the rights and obligations of a parish church community. Parishioners should be made aware what their membership entails and how it could help them to become more committed and mission oriented disciples. In addition, some dioceses may consider forming a diocesan team that could be tasked by the diocesan bishop with the actual overseeing of the process of parish mergers, closures and collaborations. Such a team if well trained and equipped with the necessary tools could be of great help to any pastor and parish leader assigned to minister to a parish community or communities in transition. The details regarding the team's role, authority, and the modus operandi could be worked out between all interested parties involved in this process.

It would also be of great help for the success of this process to ask all priests from each deanery for their honest input and recommendations. They are fully aware which parishes should be merged, closed or enter into a collaboration model of parish ministry. Lay and ordained parish leaders actively involved in parish life and ministry have the advantage of knowing peoples' perceptions, attitudes, convictions and beliefs. Their knowledge and pastoral experience should be taken seriously into account from the early planning stages of parish reconfiguration until it's actual implementation.

Last but not least, an honest evaluation of the entire process must be done, and it should be done not only towards the final stages of the process but during the course of developing and implementing a plan for parish reconfiguration. By-monthly or quarterly meetings between the bishop, diocesan officials, pastors and parish leaders ought to be an integral part of this endeavor. Listening to the struggles and challenges connected with this process would not only provide a healthy forum to voice the different needs but also it could become a source of ongoing support and practical solutions used to improve the process and its implementation. Much wisdom and practical insights could be gained from such gatherings which could be applied in various parish situations connected with structural changes.

Concluding Remarks

The Catholic people in the United States are quite mobile today, and they have been on the move for a few decades now. This trend affecting the demographics of the Catholic population will most likely continue into the future. The Northeast and the Midwest are no longer the bastions of Catholicism in the United States. Many Catholics are living now on the west coast and in the deep south of the United States. While thousands of parishes are being closed and merged in the Northeast and Midwest parts of the country, the formation of the mega churches in other areas of the United States continues to grow significantly. This is definitely the sign of our times. Furthermore, it is a sign that should not be underestimated. While we can not stop the migration of the Catholic population to the west and the south parts of the United States, we can help those experiencing the sad reality of parish closures or mergers to look at parish structural changes from a different perspective. Change whether positive or negative is never easy. Very often changes in parish structures create fear, suspicion and the anxiety of the unknown. However, sometimes change is absolutely necessary, not just for the sake of survival but also to grow and to thrive as human beings and as disciples of the Lord. Change in parish structures is capable of breathing new life into a faith community and helping the many diverse members to become fully committed intentional disciples. No matter what parish structural changes we may experience, may we never forget that we have been called as members of the Body of Christ to create welcoming parish communities where all of

God's people are loved and respected because they are the face of God who lives among us.

Appendix A.
Memorandum from Ronny E. Jenkins, General Secretary

Office of the General Secretary

3211 FOURTH STREET NE · WASHINGTON DC 20017-1194 · 202-541-3100 · FAX 202-541-3166

Cardinal Timothy M. Dolan
Archbishop of New York
President

Monsignor Ronny E. Jenkins, J.C.D.
General Secretary

Msgr. J. Brian Bransfield, S.T.D.
Linda D. Hunt, M.S.
Anthony R. Picarello, Esq.
Associate General Secretaries

MEMORANDUM

To: All Bishops

From: Reverend Monsignor Ronny E. Jenkins, *General Secretary*

Date: May 15, 2013

Subject: *Circular Letter from the Congregation for the Clergy Providing
Procedural Guidelines Related to Parish Restructuring*

Your Eminence / Your Excellency:

At the request of His Eminence Timothy Cardinal Dolan, Archbishop of New York and President, I have the pleasure to convey to you the attached letter of April 30, 2013 (Prot. No. 20131348), sent to Cardinal Dolan by His Eminence Mauro Cardinal Piacenza, Prefect of the Congregation for the Clergy, along with a Circular Letter from the Congregation providing "Procedural Guidelines for the Modification of Parishes, the Closure or Relegation of Churches to Profane but not Sordid Use, and the Alienation of the Same."

You will note that it is the Prefect's ardent hope that the summaries and jurisprudence described in the Guidelines will be of assistance to you when implementing these three distinct canonical processes, in your ongoing solicitude for the particular church that has been entrusted to your care.

Should you, or a member of your staff, have any questions about these materials, please do not hesitate to contact Ms. Siobhan M. Verbeek, J.C.L. (202-541-3016; sverbeek@usccb.org), our Director of Canonical Affairs, for further assistance.

Thank you for your kind attention to this memorandum.

Appendix B.
Letter from Cardinal Mauro Piacenza, Prefect
with Procedural Guidelines for the Modification of Parishes

CONGREGATIO
PRO CLERICIS

Vatican City, 30 April 2013

Prot. No. 20131348

His Eminence Timothy Cardinal Dolan
President
United States Conference of Catholic Bishops
3211 Fourth Street, N. E.
Washington, D.C. 20017-1194
UNITED STATES OF AMERICA

Your Eminence,

I am pleased to present to you the attached letter from the Congregation for the Clergy (Prot. No. 20131348). Addressed to all Ordinaries, it deals with the topic of the modification of parishes, the closure or relegation of churches to profane but not sordid use, and the proposed alienation of formerly sacred edifices.

It is my fervent hope that this letter will provide the necessary clarity and guidance in order to assist Ordinaries in their fulfillment of the duties with which the Lord and His Church have entrusted them.

Taking this opportunity to renew my sentiments of esteem and collegial affection, I remain

Sincerely yours in Christ,

Mauro Cardinal Piacenza
Prefect

Congregazione per il Clero - 00120 Città del Vaticano - Tel. 06/69884151 · Fax: 06/69884845

CONGREGATIO
PRO CLERICIS

Vatican City, 30 April 2013

Prot. No. 20131348

To the Eminent, Most Excellent, and Reverend Ordinaries
at their Sees

Your Eminence, Your Excellency,

The Congregation for the Clergy is aware of the significant care and pastoral solicitude with which Bishops have approached the modification of parishes (cf. can. 515 §2) and the relegation to profane use or even the simple closure of churches (cf. can. 1222 §2). Despite their best efforts, however, various difficulties concerning these questions have arisen in recent years, both for Bishops and for the faithful. In an effort to provide helpful guidance and thereby to prevent many of the difficulties heretofore experienced, this Dicastery presents the attached descriptions of the canonical procedures and jurisprudence concerning the above-mentioned processes.

Before proceeding to more specific information, some preliminary observations will prove helpful. First, it is necessary to distinguish clearly between three separate and distinct canonical processes: (1) the modification of parishes, (2) the relegation to profane use and/or the permanent closure of churches, and (3) the alienation of current or former sacred edifices. Each process has its own procedures, and each must be followed carefully and correctly. It should be noted that no process at all is required to close a church temporarily, such as for repairs. The same is true for restricting its use by such things as eliminating the celebration of Sunday Mass, provided that the church remain open for the access of the faithful (cf. can. 1214).

Secondly, when treating the modification of parishes and the relegation or closure of churches, there is a need for much greater clarity in distinguishing the juridic person of a diocese from the juridic person of a parish. Nowhere is this more apparent than in questions concerning the ownership of churches, and who is responsible for their upkeep. Likewise, it should be noted that some commonly-used terms in these processes, e.g., "suppression", have both a broad non-technical meaning as well as a precise canonical meaning. In order to avoid unnecessary confusion, it is best in canonical documents to avoid the non-technical use of such terms.

In determining whether or not the required just cause is present in the case of a proposed parish modification (cf. can. 515 §2) or the required grave cause in the case of church closure and relegation (cf. can. 1222 §2), each case must be considered separately. Although the Bishop may take into consideration the needs of surrounding parishes or even that of the diocese as a whole, he must always motivate his decree with a cause that is specific, i.e., *ad rem*, to the individual parish or church under consideration.

Lastly, each administrative decision must be enacted by a separate written decree, issued and lawfully communicated at the time that the decision is given. Because the just cause for a parish modification and the grave cause for the relegation or closure of a church are not the same, decisions regarding these processes should be issued in separate decrees.

In a spirit of fraternal collaboration, keeping in mind the responsibilities incumbent upon every Diocesan Bishop, and desiring always the good of the Church, I take this opportunity to renew my sentiments of esteem and collegial affection, and I remain

Sincerely yours in Christ,

Mauro Cardinal Piacenza
Prefect

✠ Celso Morga Iruzubieta
Titular Archbishop of Alba marittima
Secretary

with Enclosure

CONGREGATIO PRO CLERICIS

**Procedural Guidelines for the Modification of Parishes,
the Closure or Relegation of Churches to Profane but not Sordid Use,
and the Alienation of the Same**

1. *Modification of parishes*

   a) The relevant canons are chiefly can. 515, and also cann. 50, 51, 120, 121, 122, 123, 127, and 166.

   b) A parish is a community of the faithful which, being a juridic person *ipso iure*, is perpetual by its nature (cf. can. 120 §1, and can. 515 §§1, 3). It cannot be extinguished or even notably altered without just cause.

   c) There are four possible types of parish modifications. They are known by a variety of terms, sometimes interchangeably, in the various languages, leading to imprecision in decrees and other canonical documents. Such documents, however, cannot allow for imprecision. As an example, all four of these types of modifications are occasionally referred to as "suppressions", but it is clearly best to limit the use of that term in canonical documents to the fourth type, so as to avoid confusion. Likewise, the type of extinctive union intended should be clearly indicated in a decree. The four types of modifications are:
      i. extinctive union: (sometimes known as merger)
         A and B unite to form C, only C remains (cf. can. 121)
      ii. extinctive union: (sometimes also known as merger, or as amalgamation)
         A is subsumed into B, only B remains (by analogy to can. 121)
      iii. total division:
         A is divided into B and C, only B and C remain (cf. can. 122)
      iv. suppression:
         A is extinguished ... nothing remains (cf. can. 123)

   d) Since parishes are communities of the faithful, territorial parishes as a general rule can only be united or divided (cf. cann. 121 and 122). Although sometimes personal parishes are truly suppressed (cf. can. 123), they are ordinarily united or divided, either in connection to another personal parish or even to a territorial parish.

   e) The authority competent to erect, suppress, or notably alter parishes is the diocesan Bishop or those equivalent to him in law (cf. cann. 381.§2, 368, and 515 §2). He is competent to judge the existence of the required just cause, but his judgment must conform to ecclesiastical jurisprudence.

   f) According to this jurisprudence, the principal motivation for modifying a parish is a concern for souls (*Christus Dominus* no. 32) and this modification should be undertaken when the good of the faithful requires it (*Apostolorum Successores*, no. 214, which is listed as no. 215 in the Italian text).

g) Jurisprudence indicates that an extinctive union or suppression should be the last choice when dealing with various problems affecting parochial life, insofar as other possible remedies should have been at least considered beforehand and ruled out.

h) Furthermore, jurisprudence acknowledges that the diocesan Bishop can and sometimes should consider the good of the whole diocese in making his decision. Nonetheless, the reason(s) for modifying a particular parish must be relevant to that individual parish, i.e., the cause must be *ad rem*. Generalized or diocesan motivations alone cannot justify the modification of a specific parish.

i) Before rendering his decision, the Bishop must seek out the necessary information and, insofar as possible, hear those whose rights could be injured (cf. can. 50). Before consulting the members of the Presbyteral Council, which is required for validity, he must first provide them with all relevant information, lawfully convoke the Council (cf. cann. 127 and 166), and then he himself must consult the members regarding each individual parish modification which has been proposed. The consultation must be genuine, and should consider relevant arguments both for and against the proposed modifications.

j) Any decree modifying a parish must be issued in writing at the time that the decision is given and then lawfully communicated without delay. The period of time during which hierarchical recourse may be presented begins with the lawful notification of the decree (cf. can. 1734 §2). In addition, the decree must mention at least in summary form the just cause(s) for the decision (cf. can. 51).

k) The decree must clearly define the criteria for membership in all parishes affected by the modification.

l) The decree must likewise provide for the disposition of temporal goods in accord with law, and must respect the intentions of donors (cf. cann. 121, 122, and 123). Jurisprudence has clearly established that when parishes are modified, the temporal goods are to follow the people.

2. Closure of churches / Relegation of churches to profane but sordid use

a) The relevant canons are chiefly cann. 1214 and 1222, and also cann. 50, 51, 127, and 166.

b) Regardless of which juridic person owns a sacred edifice, or of the extent to which it is open, or of the popular designation by which it is called, e.g. a "mission", "chapel of devotion", "oratory", or "worship site", the law understands a church to be any sacred edifice designated for divine worship to which the faithful have the right of entry for the exercise of divine worship, especially public worship (cf. can. 1214).

c) There is a clear disposition both in law and in tradition that a sacred edifice which has been given over perpetually for divine worship should retain that sacred character if at all possible, and only a grave reason to the contrary is sufficient to justify relegating a church to profane but not sordid use (cf. can. 1222 §2). Even more so, altars do not lose their dedication or blessing when the church does, and can never be turned over to profane use for any reason (cf. cann. 1212 and 1238).

d) It is well established in ecclesiastical jurisprudence that merely to close a church permanently, even without any intention to turn it over to profane use, is juridically equivalent to relegating it to profane use. Consequently, one cannot lawfully permanently close a church without first employing the provisions of can. 1222 §2, with the corollary that in the absence of applying the provisions of can. 1222 §2, the church is to remain open.

e) The authority competent to relegate a church to profane but not sordid use according to the norm of can. 1222 §2 is the diocesan Bishop or those equivalent to him in law (cf. cann. 381§2, 368, and 515 §2). He is competent to judge the existence of the required grave cause, but his judgment must conform to ecclesiastical jurisprudence.

f) To assess the gravity of a cause, each case must be considered individually, weighing the whole context of the situation. At times, the gravity of a cause will arise only from a combination of just causes, each insufficient in itself, but which together manifest the seriousness of the situation.

g) When considering questions of finances, the relevant financial need is that of the juridic person which owns the church and is therefore responsible for it. Furthermore, it must be demonstrated that other reasonable sources of funding or assistance have been considered and found lacking or inadequate.

h) Because churches can remain sacred edifices even though they are only occasionally or even rarely used, jurisprudence has established that the following reasons in themselves do not constitute grave cause:
   i.   a general plan of the diocese to reduce the number of churches .
   ii. the church is no longer needed
   iii. the parish has been suppressed
   iv. the number of parishioners has decreased
   v.   closure will not harm the good of souls
   vi. a desire to promote the unity of the parish
   vii. some potential future cause that has not actually happened yet

i) Before rendering his decision, the Bishop must seek out the necessary proofs and, insofar as possible, hear those whose rights could be injured (cf. can. 50). In addition, before consulting the members of the Presbyteral Council, which is required for validity, he must first provide them with all relevant information, lawfully convoke the Council (cf. cann. 127 and 166), and then he himself must consult the members regarding each individual relegation which has been proposed. The consultation must be genuine, and should consider relevant arguments both for and against the proposed relegation. He must also obtain the consent of those who claim legitimate rights in the edifice (cf. cann. 1222 §2 and 127) and verify that the good of souls will suffer no harm (cf. can 1222 §2).

j) The Bishop must give his decision by means of a written decree issued in writing at the time when the decision is given and then lawfully communicated without delay. The period of time during which hierarchical recourse may be presented begins with the lawful notification of the decree (cf. can. 1734 §2). In addition, the decree must mention at least in summary form the grave cause(s) for the decision (cf. can. 51).

3. *Alienation of churches*

a) The relevant canons are chiefly cann. 1291-1298, and also cann. 50, 51, 127, and 166.

b) The canons on alienation apply not only to the actual sale of an edifice, but also to other transactions which could harm the stable patrimony of the juridic person which owns it (cf. can. 1295).

c) If after it is alienated, a church will remain in use as a Catholic place for divine worship to which the faithful have a continued right of access, e.g., by sale to a different Ritual Church *sui iuris*, it should not be relegated to profane use prior to the alienation. In all other situations, however, it must be relegated to profane but not sordid use prior to being alienated.

d) If it becomes necessary to alienate the edifice, various options, listed in decreasing order of preference are:
   i.   for continued use as a place of Catholic worship (non-relegated)
   ii.   for use as a place for the exercise of other Catholic apostolates or ministries
   iii. for profane but not sordid use in keeping with the dignity of the edifice as a former church
   iv.   demolition of the edifice, recovering the land

e) Under no circumstances can the edifice be alienated for use inconsistent with its inherent dignity as a former church. Contractual agreements are to be put in place to safeguard this point in civil law as well as canonically.

f) Furthermore, the competent authority must assure that there is no reasonable possibility of scandal or loss of the faithful which will result from the proposed alienation.

g) Prior to alienation, all sacred objects, relics, sacred furnishings, stained-glass windows, bells, confessionals, altars, etc. are to be removed for use in other sacred edifices or to be stored in ecclesiastical custody. Because altars can never be turned over to profane use, if they cannot be removed, they must be destroyed (cf. cann. 1212 and 1238).

h) Regarding the procedures for alienation:
   i.   When the value of the edifice lies beneath the minimum amount established by the Episcopal Conference, the competent authority is the pastor or that defined by the statutes, unless particular law determines otherwise. That authority must have at least a just cause to alienate the edifice.
   ii.   When the value of the edifice lies between minimum and maximum amounts, the competent authority must have a just cause for alienation, together with written appraisal by experts (cf. can. 1293). For juridic persons which are not subject to the Bishop, the competent authority is identified by the statues. In all other cases, it is the diocesan Bishop, who must also have the consent of the diocesan Finance Council, the consent of the College of Consultors, and the consent of interested parties (cf. cann. 1292 §1, 127, and 166).
   iii. When value of the edifice exceeds the maximum amount established by the Episcopal Conference, or if the edifice was given by vow, or is precious for artistic or historical reasons, then the competent authority, either that identified by the statues or the diocesan Bishop, must also have the consent of the Holy See (cf. can. 1292 §2).

104

Appendix C.
Diocese of Youngstown Reconfiguration Plan 2010

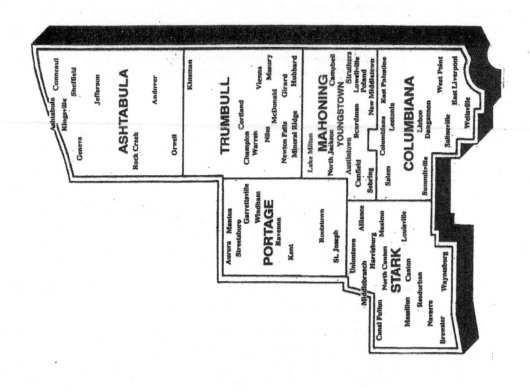

DIOCESE OF YOUNGSTOWN
FEBRUARY 24, 2010

PROPOSED
PARISH
DRAFT

ASHTABULA DEANERY

First Set of numbers represents the Parish Reported households
Second Set of Numbers represents households from Catholic Charities Records

SINGLE UNITS

Assumption, Geneva - 725   (706)

St. Mary/St. Francis Cabrini, Conneaut - 927 (862)

COLLABORATIVE UNITS

Our Lady of Victory, Andover   342 (272)
St. Patrick, Kinsman
  1 – Pastor
  2 – Parishes

St. Joseph, Jefferson   490   (416)
St. Andrew, Sheffield
  1 – Pastor
  2 – Parishes

St. Mary, Orwell   592   (553)
Sacred Heart, Rock Creek
  1 – Pastor
  2 – Parishes

MERGED UNIT

St. Joseph, Ashtabula
Our Lady of Miracles, Mission
Mother of Sorrows, Ashtabula
Our Lady of Mount Carmel, Ashtabula   2797   (2709)

The three city parishes and one mission, merge into one parish with two worship sites, served by a pastor, parochial vicar, and ministerial team.

The Hispanic community will be ministered to within the structure.

Present Number of Clergy 7

Proposed Number of Clergy 7

COLUMBIANA DEANERY

First Set of numbers represents the Parish Reported households
Second Set of Numbers represents households
from Catholic Charities Records

COLLABORATIVE UNITS

St. Jude, Columbiana
Our Lady of Lourdes, East Palestine   } 937 (970)   1 – Pastor
2 – Parishes

St. Paul, Salem
St. Patrick, Leetonia   } 1600 (1612)   1 – Pastor
2 – Parishes

MERGED UNITS

St. George, Lisbon *
St. Agatha Mission, West Point
St. John, Summitville *
St. Philip Neri, Dungannon *
St. Patrick, Salineville (Parish suppressed)   } 398 (331)   1 – Pastor
3 – Parishes *

St. Agatha Mission will
be merged into
St. George

St. Aloysius, East Liverpool
Immaculate Conception, Wellsville   } 1085 (947)   1 – Pastor
1 – Parish
St. Ann, East Liverpool   1 – Worship Site

Present Number of Clergy 8

Proposed Number of Clergy 4

MAHONING NORTH & SOUTH DEANERIES

First Set of numbers represents the Parish Reported households
Second Set of Numbers represents households from Catholic Charities Records

SINGLE UNITS	MERGED UNITS	MERGED UNITS	MERGED UNITS	MERGED UNITS	MERGED UNITS
Immaculate Heart of Mary, Austintown - 1580 (1360)	St. Elizabeth / St. John the Baptist / St. Jos. the Provider / St. Lucy / St. Rose of Lima	SS Cyril & Methodius / Holy Name / St. Matthias	St. Casimir / St. Stanislaus	St. Anthony / Our Lady of Mt. Carmel	St. Stephen of Hungary / Our Lady of Hungary / SS Peter & Paul
St. Joseph, Austintown – 1957 (1716)					
St. Charles, Boardman – 3092 (3081)	1539 (1488)	1421 (1414)	415 (367)	1356 (1369)	649 (606)
St. Luke, Boardman – 963 (1012)	1 - Pastor / 1 - Parish / 2 - Worship Sites / Creation of a Pastoral Team	1 - Pastor / 1 - Parish / 1 - Worship Site	1 - Pastor / 1 - Parish / 1 - Worship Site / Pastor to have add'l responsibilities	1 - Pastor / 1 - Parish / 1 - Worship Site	1 - Pastor / 1 - Parish / 1 - Worship Site
St. Michael, Canfield – 1750 (1601)					
St. Paul the Apostle, New Middletown – 950 (915)	Hispanic Community will be ministered to within this structure				
Holy Family, Poland – 2075 (2143)					
St. Christine, Youngstown – 2528 (2643)					
St. Dominic, Youngstown – 1055 (1039)					

MAHONING NORTH & SOUTH DEANERIES

First Set of numbers represents the Parish Reported households
Second Set of Numbers represents households from Catholic Charities Records

SINGLE UNIT	MERGE UNIT	MERGE UNIT	MERGE UNIT
St. Columba Youngstown – **669** *(644)*	St. Nicholas, Struthers	Immaculate Conception Youngstown	St. Catherine, Lake Milton
Holy Rosary Lowellville – **620** *(630)*	Holy Trinity, Struthers	Sacred Heart, Youngstown	St. James. North Jackson
St. Edward – **460** *(426)*	**1 - Pastor**	**1 - Pastor**	**1 - Pastor**
St. Brendan – **824** *(717)*	**1 - Parish**	**1 - Parish**	**1 - Parish**
St. Patrick – **685** *(668)*	**1 Worship Site(s)**	**1 - Worship Site**	**2 - Worship Site(s)**
2177 *(1840)*		**690** *(538)*	**464** *(527)*

Present Number of Clergy 30

Proposed Number of Clergy .... 25 *(Including Parochial Vicars)*

Numbers do not include St. Dominic

PORTAGE DEANERY

First Set of numbers represents the Parish Reported households
Second Set of Numbers represents households from Catholic Charities Records

SINGLE UNITS

Our Lady of Perpetual Help, Aurora – 1478 (1383)

St. Joseph, Mantua – 1050 (666)

St. Joan of Arc, Streetsboro – 975 (877)

Immaculate Conception, Ravenna – 982 (955)

St. Patrick, Kent – 1080 (977)

University Parish Newman Center, Kent – 215 (222)
Number of Catholic Students

COLLABORATIVE UNITS

St. Joseph, Randolph
St. Peter of the Fields, Rootstown } 1281 (1246) 1 – Pastor
                                       2 – Parishes

St. Ambrose, Garrettsville
St. Michael, Windham } 462 (516)
                        1 – Pastor
                        2 – Parishes

Present Number of Clergy 10

Proposed Number of Clergy 8

110

STARK DEANERY

First Set of numbers represents the Parish Reported households
Second Set of Numbers represents households from Catholic Charities Records

SINGLE UNITS

SS. Philip & James - **683** *(655)*

St. Joan of Arc - **1642** *(1542)*

St. Joseph - **1194** *(1233)*

St. Michael - **2594** *(2559)*

Little Flower - **1108** *(1169)*

St. James - **325** *(311)*

St. Paul, North Canton - **2843** *(2570)*

Holy Spirit - **560** *(554)*

St. Mary, **1765** *(1747)*

St. Joseph - **1106** *(870)*

St. Barbara - **900** *(953)*

St. Louis, Louisville - **1067** *(975)*

MERGED UNITS

St. Joseph, Alliance / Regina Coeli / St. Ann — **1398** *(1400)* — 1- Pastor, 2- Worship Sites, 1 - Parish
1- additional priest with added responsibilities

St. Theresa, Brewster / St. Clement, Navarre — **491** *(478)* — 1- Pastor, 2 - Worship Sites, 1 - Parish

St. Peter, Canton / St. Benedict, Canton — **1506** *(1554)* — 1- Pastor, 1 - Worship Site, 1 - Parish

All Saints / St. Anthony — **933** *(801)* — 1 - Parish, 1 - Pastor, 1 - Worship Site
Hispanic Community will be ministered to within this structure

St. Mary / St. John — **1263** *(945)* — 1 - Pastor, 1 - Worship Site, 1 - Parish

Sacred Heart of Mary / St. Joseph, Maximo — **592** *(524)* — 1 - Parish, 1 - Pastor, 1 - Worship Site

Our Lady of Peace / St. Paul Canton — **1004** *(1300)* — 1 - Parish, 1 - Pastor, 1- Worship Site

Present Number of Clergy 27
Proposed Number of Clergy 23

Appendix D.
Strategic Planning Committee for Diocese of Youngstown Plan

Strategic Planning Executive Committee

Rev. Monsignor John A. Zuraw
Reverend Bradford Helman
Reverend Bernard Bonnot
Rev. Monsignor Lewis Gaetano
Reverend Gregory Fedor
Rev. Monsignor David Rhodes

Ashtabula Deanery
Reverend Raymond Thomas, VF
Dwight Beebe
Helen Orgovan

Columbiana Deanery
Reverend Thomas Eisweirth, VF
Sue DeJane
Sr. Joan Franklin, OP

Mahoning South Deanery
Reverend Nicholas Shori, VF
Barb Zorn
Todd Bury

Mahoning North Deanery
Reverend Stephen Popovich, VF
Thomas Metzinger
Marge O'Malley

Portage Deanery
Reverend Richard Pentello, VF
Michalene Murphy
Deacon Russell Brode

Trumbull Deanery
Reverend Donald King, VF
Terry Supancic
James Pipino

Stark Deanery
Reverend James Clarke, VF
Deacon Ron Reolfi
Sr. Karen Lindenberger, OSF/T
Frank Monaco
Henry Kappel

George Garchar - Demographic Consultant
Lou Jacquet - Communications Consultant
Reverend James Daprile - Theological Consultant

Appendix E.
Terminology for Diocese of Youngstown Plan

TERMINOLOGY

PARISH:

A parish is extinguished by the law itself only if no Catholic Community any longer exists in its territory, or no pastoral activity has taken place for one hundred years. (Canon 120.1) When a parish is suppressed by competent authority in reality the still existing community is actually merged into the neighboring community of Christ's faithful.

In the case where the portion of the Christian faithful is relocation among pre-existing or newly created parishes, the patrimony and obligations of the suppressed parish must follow the Faithful in equitable and proportionate fashion.

CLOSED PARISH:

A canonical declaration by the Diocesan Bishop in consultation with the Presbyteral Council that a parish ceases to exist. Parish members join one of the neighboring parishes.

CLUSTER PARISH:

- A grouping of two or more parishes served by one or more priests.
- The parishes retain separate identities (i.e. buildings, pastoral and financial councils, day to day administration of the parish)
- Collaborate in sharing of staff, resources and programming (i.e. sacramental preparation, religious education, adult faith formation, youth ministry)
- A pastoral ministry coordinator could handle much of the day to day administration of the parish.
- Distances between parishes may dictate the level of collaborative programs.

MERGED PARISH:

- A parish joined with two or more parishes to form a single new or consolidated parish. Canonically, one new parish is created.
- There is only one set of councils: One pastoral council and one financial council.
- One staff at a common, central location.
- Standardized committees, policies and procedures.
- This structure allows for the community to maintain multiple churches/worship sites.

CHAPEL:

There are several types of chapels, including chapels of adoration inside parish churches or sanctified areas of other buildings such as hospitals. For the purpose of this study, a chapel is a church that is dependent upon, and subordinate to a parish.

Appendix F.
Time Table for Diocese of Youngstown Plan

TIME TABLE ON PARISH PLANNING

I. Announce the need for a change - **Winter/Spring 2008**

II. Collect pertinent information - **Fall/Winter 2008**

III. Craft vision/mission statement - **Spring of 2009**

IV. Determine yardstick for measuring how well parishes reflect the vision - **Spring of 2009**

V. Compare and contrast self-evaluations with established criteria - **(May of 2009 Deanery Meetings)**

VI. Lead parish to see its realistic needs and actively participate in creative planning **(Two Deanery Meetings, one in July and one in September 2009)**

VII. Executive Committee makes recommendations for reconfiguration **(Fall to early winter 2009-10)**

VIII. Bishop makes final decision **(Winter to early spring 2010)**

IX. Decisions are made public **(Pentecost 2010)**

X. Implementation Phase Begins - **(Ongoing)**

Appendix G.
Consolidation Plan for St. Mary and St. Joseph Parhishes, Newton Falls, OH

Consolidation Plan
for

ST. MARY &
ST. JOSEPH PARISHES

Newton Falls, Ohio

January 16, 2007

Rev. Msgr. Robert Siffrin,

The following report presents recent data and statistics concerning the financial status and viability of St. Mary's Parish in Newton Falls, Ohio.

In July of 2006, an Ad Hoc Committee was formed by the joint Parish Pastoral Council of St. Mary & St. Joseph Churches to determine the feasibility of combining both parishes in order to meet their present financial and spiritual needs. This Committee was charged with the responsibility of gathering and evaluating data and presenting the Council with their findings and recommendations.

In actuality, the consolidation of our churches began in 1966 when Bishop Malone declared that St. Joseph Parish should collaborate with St. Mary Parish in the building of a new Catholic elementary school. Since that time we have been working together for the betterment of the school and churches. The majority of parishioners in both parishes have been looking forward to the day when we can work together with a single voice for the growth of the Roman Catholic Church in Newton Falls.

It is our goal to equitably consolidate all the assets of each parish under one name and one advisory board with a vision to the future growth and solvency of one single church.

St. Joseph's is the larger parish with some moderate growth and a more dynamic source of income due to the number of families. St. Joseph has an active program for religious education and community building as well as a parish cemetery.

A few months ago all parishioners received a survey in order to give them an opportunity to voice their opinion about their vision for the future of Sts. Mary & Joseph Parishes as well as to see their attitude toward consolidation of both parishes. The results of the survey have been presented to all parishioners and are included in this report.

The unanimous recommendation of the Ad Hoc committee supported by the vast majority of parishioners is that the prompt consolidation of both parishes is absolutely necessary in order for us to survive financially and grow spiritually. The Joint Parish Pastoral Council and the Ad Hoc Committee have concurred that in order to be as welcoming as possible and to preserve the strong heritage from St. Mary Parish, we should combine the names of the two Parishes as well as the resources. The school has operated under the name of SS. Mary & Joseph for many years, so it is only a logical progression that the combined parishes adopt the same name.

As the present spiritual leader of both communities, I am convinced that now is the time for the actual consolidation to take place. For many years both parish communities have been aware of the inevitability of consolidation, and the Catholic faithful in Newton Falls have reached a point where they will be willing and supportive of the unity of both Parishes under a common name. It is absolutely essential that the diocesan response in this matter be made without delay.

We do not wish to miss this momentum in the lives of both parishes. I am convinced that once the actual consolidation takes place, our Catholic community in Newton Falls will be stronger and more viable in the spiritual and financial sense.

Respectfully,

Rev. Matthew Maciej Mankowski, M. A., M. Div.

St. Mary & St. Joseph Ad Hoc Committee

Names removed for privacy

117

St. Mary & St. Joseph Survey Results

Out of 710 surveys that were sent out, 24% of St. Joseph parishioners responded, and 26% of St. Mary parishioners responded. Following are some results of the survey.

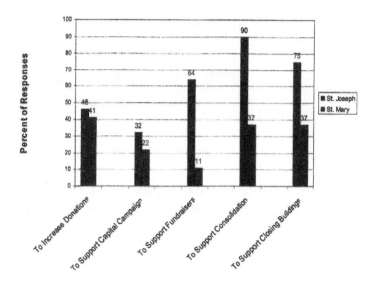

The chart above depicts positive responses to options presented to the parishes aimed at relieving our financial distress. The numbers represent the *percentage* of the total responses received from either parish that support each proposed option.

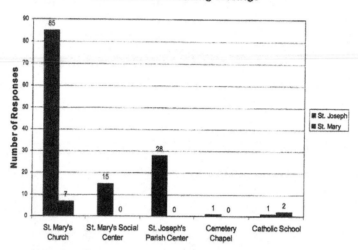

The chart above represents the *total number* of responses from either parish that support closing certain buildings that are currently used by the parishes.

Comments and suggestions included with the surveys demonstrated many common sentiments as illustrated below:

➢ The Churches must unite. Considering the present financial situation of both parishes, the loss of jobs in our area, and the fact that many of our parishioners live on a fixed income, we need to look at complete consolidation.
➢ We should keep the school open to teach the younger generation about our faith, morals, and Catholic traditions.
➢ Our financial problems are a reflection of spiritual needs as well as a lack of stewardship in our parish.
➢ It is important to our school and parishes to keep St. Mary's Social Hall open for Bingo, Parish Events and school activities.

> A significant number of parishioners will support a parish capital campaign to do the necessary renovations at St. Joseph Church, church parking lots at St. Mary & St. Joseph and St. Mary Social Hall.

The Ad Hoc Committee reviewed the Parish Surveys and determined that both Parishes, as represented in the surveys, would support the following conclusions and recommendations:

Conclusions

> The Churches must unite to survive fiscally and to grow spiritually.
> Consolidation is absolutely necessary.
> SSMJ School must remain open in accordance with our Mission Statement.
> St. Mary Social Hall is needed for Bingo, Parish Events, and School Events.
> Necessary repairs and renovations will not be covered by current contribution trends.

Recommendations

> Close St. Joseph Parish Center

> Suppress St. Mary Parish and utilize the building for other needs.

> Plan a Parish Capital Campaign to cover present and future repairs and renovations.

In conclusion, the Joint Parish Pastoral Council has reviewed the data, along with the conclusions and recommendations of the Ad Hoc Committee, and has determined that the information is accurate and valid. Consolidation of the two parishes is as much a spiritual necessity as a financial one. Any vision of a spiritually vibrant and financially sound parish in the future of the Catholic Church in Newton Falls must include the combined energy, effort and resources of St. Mary and St. Joseph Parishes. Only in this manner can we hope to heal our wounds, pay off our debt, and spiritually thrive.

SS. Mary & Joseph Joint Parish Pastoral Council

Names removed for privacy

St. Mary Parish Statistics (April 2006)

Registered households...   110
Number of persons.........   170
Deaths.........................   3
Baptisms.....................   0
First Communions..........   1
Confirmations...............   3

Parish Activities and Organizations:
- Joint Finance Committee (with St. Joseph)
- Joint Parish Pastoral Council
- Joint Liturgy Committee
- Joint Christ Renews His Parish Process

St. Mary Debt as of January 16, 2007

Debt to DOY................... $37,838.13
Debt to St. Joseph............ $46,916.00
Total Debt to Date............ $84,754.13

Income/mo. – Collection & Bingo. $8,204.00
Expenses/mo........................... $10,314.00

Monthly Debt incurred................ $2110.00
Yearly Debt estimate.................. $25320.00

Appendix H.
Letter of Acceptance of Plan – Bishop Murry

OFFICE OF THE BISHOP

DIOCESE OF YOUNGSTOWN

November 5, 2007

Reverend Maciej Mankowski
St. Mary and St. Joseph Parishes
131 West Quarry Street
Newton Falls, Ohio 44444

Dear Father Mankowski:

Thank you for your formal correspondence from the Parish Council of St. Mary and St. Joseph concerning your request for a merger of the parishes. After careful consideration of the information presented by you and the Parish Council, I grant your request.

I understand that the last liturgy at St. Mary Parish will be the Feast of Christ Our King on November 24, 2008. This will be an appropriate day to thank the Lord for the many blessing he has bestowed on St. Mary and St. Joseph and to petition His guidance and strength for the new direction of the parish.

The financial and demographic issues in our area have resulted in the loss of jobs and the move of some parishioners out of the area. The drawing together of parishioners and resources can help to secure the future of the parish.

Your leadership as pastor and the support of the members of Parish Council are deeply appreciated.

The next issues for implementing this request will be the formal decision on the change of name and a financial plan for the assumption of the resources and liabilities of both parishes.

My prayers are with you and the parishioners of St. Mary and St. Joseph.

Yours in Christ,

Most Reverend George V. Murry, S.J.
Bishop of Youngstown

Appendix I.
Decree of Merger by Bishop Murry

DIOCESE OF YOUNGSTOWN

GEORGE V. MURRY, S.J.

By the Grace of God and the Apostolic See

BISHOP OF YOUNGSTOWN

DECREE OF MERGER

For eighty years, the Catholic Faithful of Saint Mary Parish in the Diocese of Youngstown have been served by Saint Mary Parish, 120 Maple Drive, Newton Falls, Ohio. During that time countless people have heard the Word of God, have worshipped and received the Sacraments of the Church in the parish community. Likewise, for eighty-five years, the Catholic Faithful of Saint Joseph Parish in the Diocese of Youngstown have been served by Saint Joseph Parish, 131 West Quarry Street, Newton Falls, Ohio. During that time countless people have heard the Word of God, have worshipped and received the Sacraments of the Church in the parish community. In an effort to reorganize the People of God in this portion of God's Kingdom, it now is necessary to make new provisions for the spiritual care of the parishioners of both Saint Mary Parish and Saint Joseph Parish.

Accordingly, having reviewed the pastoral statistics and studied facts compiled by the Diocese of Youngstown, after consultation with representatives of both parish communities, having heard the Presbyteral Council and acting in accord with canon 515, paragraph 2, of the Code of Canon Law, I hereby alter and merge Saint Mary Parish and Saint Joseph Parish. This merger shall be effective on May 13, 2008, the Feast of Our Lady of Fatima.

All parishioners of both parishes are now members of the new merged parish to be named Saint Mary and Saint Joseph Church, Newton Falls, Ohio.

All of the original registers containing records of Baptism, Confirmation, Marriage and Christian Burial hitherto preserved by both parishes are now to be faithfully preserved in the new merged parish.

All properties and assets of both parishes are now part of the amalgamation into the juridic person of Saint Mary and St. Joseph Church.

In accord with canon 1222, I have also consulted with the Presbyteral Council and now allow St. Mary Church to be used for parish offices. The Pastor will further be attentive in maintaining the sacred vessels, statues and other sacred objects of both parishes in a manner whereby their reverence is appropriately preserved within the newly merged parish.

Given at Youngstown, Ohio, this thirteenth day of May, 2008.

Most Reverend George V. Murry, S.J.
Bishop of Youngstown

Nancy Juhász
Chancellor

Linda Tedde
Notary

Appendix J.
Book Research Survey

Thank you for participating in my survey. This survey is being conducted by Rev. Matthew Mankowski for a Doctor of Ministry Research.

Please obtain your access code and follow the instructions in the cover letter.

Your feedback is very important. Please answer all questions honestly and to the best of your ability.

Fr. Matthew Mankowski

Rev. Matthew Mankowski - Doctor of Ministry Research

Informative Survey for Doctor of Ministry Research

Please answer all questions - use the next button to continue if you are completing online. If you are completing this survey on paper, please return it in the self addressed stamped envelope. This survey consists of 15 questions, one of which has several statements to evaluate. The time to complete should be less than 20 minutes.

* **1. Please enter the four digit access code listed at the top of your cover letter.**

[   ]

* **2. Please, mark one answer/category that pertains to you at the present time:**

☐ I am a Pastor

☐ I am a lay parish administrator

☐ I am a permanent deacon

☐ I am a parishioner

☐ I am a woman religious

☐ I am a man religious

* 3. I have been actively involved in my parish life in the following areas (check all that apply)

- [ ] Weekly Mass attendance
- [ ] Daily Mass attendance
- [ ] Lector
- [ ] Eucharistic Minister
- [ ] Usher
- [ ] Cantor
- [ ] Bereavement Ministry
- [ ] St Vincent DePaul (or other service organization or ministry to poor)
- [ ] Choir or Music Ministry
- [ ] Religious Education program instructor (CCD or RCIA)
- [ ] Knight of Columbus or Catholic Woman's organizations
- [ ] Parish Committees - Liturgy, Social, Stewardship, etc.
- [ ] Parish Leadership group - Pastoral Council, Finance Council, etc.
- [ ] Other (please specify)

Rev. Matthew Mankowski - Doctor of Ministry Research

Parish Affiliation

* 4. How long have you been a member of this parish?

○ less than 3 years

○ 4- 7 years

○ 8-12 years

○ 13-20 years

○ 25 - 50 years

○ over 50 years

* 5. Were you a member of the parish when the process to close/collaborate or merge began?

○ Yes

○ No

* 6. At the time the closing/collaboration or merger began, I belonged to the following parish:

○ St. John the Baptist Parish - Campbell, OH

○ St. Joseph the Provider Parish - Campbell, OH

○ St. Lucy Parish - Campbell, OH

○ St. Rosa de Lima Parish - Campbell, OH

○ St. Joseph Parish - Newton Falls, OH

○ St Mary Parish - Newton Falls, OH

○ Christ Our King Parish - Warren, OH

○ St. Joseph Parish - Warren, OH

○ St. Pius X Parish - Warren, OH

○ Other (please specify)

Rev. Matthew Mankowski - Doctor of Ministry Research

Rating Scale -Strongly Disagree to Strongly Agree

* 7. Please evaluate the following statements based on your experiences with the closing/collaboration or merger process in your parish.

	Strongly Disagree	Disagree	Neither Disagree Nor Agree	Agree	Strongly Agree
a.) I felt that the Diocese of Youngstown offered sufficient information and support to our parish <u>before</u> the process began.	○	○	○	○	○

Comments to your response above:

b.) The parishioners were well informed regarding the reasons or need for the closing/collaboration or merger to occur.	○	○	○	○	○

Comments to your response above:

c.) Sufficient information was provided by the pastor and parish leadership team regarding the parish financial standing.	○	○	○	○	○

Comments to your response above:

d.) Sufficient information was provided by the pastor and parish leadership team regarding the financial impact of the closing/collaboration or merger.	○	○	○	○	○

	Strongly Disagree	Disagree	Neither Disagree Nor Agree	Agree	Strongly Agree

Comments to your response above:

e.) Consideration was given as to the impact this would have on our parish community <u>before</u> the process began.

Comments to your response above:

f.) Parish organizations and ministries were given opportunities to provide input into the process from the beginning.

Comments to your response above:

g.) Parishioners were given sufficient time to understand the different stages of the process of closing/collaboration or merger.

Comments to your response above:

h.) A deliberate attempt was made to allow individual parishioners to ask questions and give input.

Comments to your response above:

	Strongly Disagree	Disagree	Neither Disagree Nor Agree	Agree	Strongly Agree
i.) Some parishioners felt that the decision was already made and our input was not really considered.	◯	◯	◯	◯	◯

Comments to your response above:

j.) The diocese maintained a supportive presence in our parish throughout the process from beginning to end.	◯	◯	◯	◯	◯

Comments to your response above:

k.) The implementation of the process was difficult for all parishioners.	◯	◯	◯	◯	◯

Comments to your response above:

l.) The diocese was in constant communication with the pastor and parishioners to provide support and information throughout the implementation of the process.	◯	◯	◯	◯	◯

Comments to your response above:

m.) The diocese gave careful consideration regarding the pastors ability to manage this process.	◯	◯	◯	◯	◯

	Strongly Disagree	Disagree	Neither Disagree Nor Agree	Agree	Strongly Agree

Comments to your response above:

[ ]

n.) The diocese gave careful consideration regarding the health and well being of pastors involved in this process.   ○ ○ ○ ○ ○

Comments to your response above:

[ ]

o.) Pastors were provided with training and access to consultants to assist with the process of closing/collaboration or merger.   ○ ○ ○ ○ ○

Comments to your response above:

[ ]

p.) It was evident that the diocese provided a clear sense of direction and manageable timeline for the implementation of this process.   ○ ○ ○ ○ ○

Comments to your response above:

[ ]

q.) The closing/collaboration or merger process has been successful in our parish.   ○ ○ ○ ○ ○

Comments to your response above:

[ ]

	Strongly Disagree	Disagree	Neither Disagree Nor Agree	Agree	Strongly Agree
r.) There are many positive outcomes and results from the efforts that were made in this process.	○	○	○	○	○

Comments to your response above:

s.) The diocese has assessed the impact the process has had on our parish community.	○	○	○	○	○

Comments to your response above:

t.) We receive timely communications from the Diocese on how our new parish community is progressing.	○	○	○	○	○

Comments to your response above:

u.) Various opportunities were provided to allow parishioners to grieve and mourn their loss.	○	○	○	○	○

Comments to your response above:

134

Rev. Matthew Mankowski - Doctor of Ministry Research

Please complete the following:

* **8. My ethnic background is:**

- ( ) American
- ( ) Italian
- ( ) Irish
- ( ) German
- ( ) Polish
- ( ) Slovak
- ( ) Other (please specify)

  [   ]

* **9. What is the highest level of school you have completed or the highest degree you have received?**

- ( ) Less than high school degree
- ( ) High school degree or equivalent (e.g., GED)
- ( ) Some college but no degree
- ( ) Associate degree
- ( ) Bachelor degree
- ( ) Graduate degree

* **10. What is your gender?**

- ( ) Female
- ( ) Male

* 11. What is your age?

○ 18 to 24

○ 25 to 34

○ 35 to 44

○ 45 to 54

○ 55 to 64

○ 65 to 74

○ 75 or older

12. What worked well in this process in your parish?

13. What did not work well?

14. How could this process have been improved?

15. If you would like to be contacted to discuss your responses, please list your name and phone number below. If you do not wish to be contacted, please leave blank. Thank you!

Appendix K.
Sample Letter to Pastors for Survey

Rev. Matthew Maciej Mankowski, M.A., M. Div.
Cell Phone: (330) xxx-xxxx
E-mail: xxxxxxxx@aol.com
427 East Broadway Street, Alliance, OH 44601

May 19, 2015

Dear Fr. ,

Thank you for agreeing to help me with my D. Min. Project. As I previously indicated, I would like to obtain the names, addresses and phone numbers of ten individuals from each of the four former parishes that presently constitute Christ the Good Shepherd Parish. (Please, keep those names separated in the order corresponding with their previous parish membership.) My research is in need of people who were part of the restructuring process before, during and after May 28, 2010 when the Diocese of Youngstown had announced the reconfiguration plan. Lifetime members and people who experienced the planning and the implementation phases of this process are the best candidates for this research.

Please, assure them of confidentiality which I take very seriously per our academic standards and the state and federal laws. Enclosed please find a copy of a cover letter and the actual survey which I would like your parishioners to complete and mail back to me by July 4, 2015. The survey may be taken in written form or online at https://www.surveymonkey.com/s/Mankowski. Please, forward 40 names and addresses of your various parishioners to my personal assistant, by June10, 2015. My assisitant will send a cover letter along with the printed survey and a self-addressed stamped envelope to all individuals who have been designated by you as potential candidates for this study. I am very grateful for your willingness to help me with my research. If you have any questions, comments or concerns, please, do not hesitate to let me know. If I can be of assistance to you in the future, please, contact me by phone or mail and I will help in any way, shape or form.

Sincerely in Christ I remain,

Rev. Matthew Maciej Mankowski

Appendix L.
Cover Letter and Response Card to Prospective Parishioner Respondents

Rev. Matthew Maciej Mankowski, M.A., M. Div., D. Min. Cand.
Work Phone: (330) 821-5760
Cell Phone: (330) XXX - XXXX
E-mail: xxxxxxxx@aol.com
427 East Broadway Street, Alliance, OH 44601

Web page:
https://www.surveymonkey.com/s/Mankowski

Access Code: 4315

May 20, 201

Dear Friend in Christ,

My name is Fr. Matthew Mankowski and I am a student priest pursuing a Doctorate Degree at St. Mary Seminary in Wickliffe, OH. Presently, I am also a pastor of St. Joseph Parish in Alliance, Ohio. As a part of my doctoral studies I need to conduct a survey among a select group of parishioners from different parishes in the Diocese of Youngstown, Ohio, who have been involved in the process of merging, closing or collaborating of parishes.

You have been recommended by your pastor as a possible candidate for this survey. I would like to invite you to please, consider participating in this important survey. The purpose of this research is to study and analyze how the process of merging, closing or collaborating of parishes, has been introduced, implemented and executed in the Diocese of Youngstown, Ohio. Your answers will be of great help to me as I try to develop a pastoral plan for pastors and parish leaders who may be asked to be a part of such a process in the future.

Your opinio and **honesty** are very important to this study. Your participation will involve answering several questions which should take no more a few minutes of your time. You can take this survey online at **https://www.surveymonkey.com/s/Mankowski** by entering your access code printed in the left top corner of this cover letter or by filling out the paper form survey included in this mailing. Please, know that your name will be kept confidential at all times. In my study and analysis of the survey I will use made up names for all participants.

The results of this survey will be used in writing for my doctoral studies in order to develop a pastoral plan for Catholic parishes in transition. There is also a possibility that I may publish this study or refer to it in published writings in the future. In this event, I will continue to use pseudonyms (as described above) and I may alter some identifying details in order to further protect your anonymity.

If there is a need for an additional one-on-one interview, I will contact you personally and I will ask you to consider such a possibility. There are no known risks or discomforts associated with this research.

Please, know that I am very grateful for your time and willingness to be a part of this study. May God continue to bless you and watch over you in the days that are yet to come. Thank you for your kind consideration to respond to this survey.

Sincerely Yours in Christ,

Fr. Matthew Mankowski

Title of Study:
Journeying Together in Christ as a Viable Parish Community: A Pastoral Plan for Merging, Closing and Collaborating Parishes Based on Selected Case Studies from the Diocese of Youngstown, OH.

A Survey conducted by Fr. Matthew Mankowski

Voluntary Participation
Your participation in this research study is voluntary. You may choose not to participate and you may withdraw your consent to participate at any time. You will not be penalized in any way should you decide not to participate or to withdraw from this study.

Contact information
If you have any questions or concerns about this study or if any problems arise, please contact Fr. Matthew Mankowski at St. Joseph Parish, Alliance, OH at his work phone 330-821-5760 or his cell phone 330-XXX-XXXX. If Fr. Mankowski is unavailable, please, ask for my personal assistant.

140

Participation Intention Card

☐ YES, I **WILL** participate in the survey.

   A) _____ Online
   B) _____ Written Form

☐ NO, I will **NOT** participate in the survey.

Participation Intention Card

☐ YES, I **WILL** participate in the survey.

   A) _____ Online
   B) _____ Written Form

☐ NO, I will **NOT** participate in the survey.

Participation Intention Card

☐ YES, I **WILL** participate in the survey.

   A) _____ Online
   B) _____ Written Form

☐ NO, I will **NOT** participate in the survey.

Participation Intention Card

☐ YES, I **WILL** participate in the survey.

   A) _____ Online
   B) _____ Written Form

☐ NO, I will **NOT** participate in the survey.

Appendix M.
Follow up Letter

Rev. Matthew Maciej Mankowski, M.A., M. Div., D. Min. Cand.
Work Phone: (330) 821-5760
Cell Phone: (330) XXX-XXXX
E-mail: xxxxxxxx@aol.com
427 East Broadway Street, Alliance, OH 44601

July 17, 2015

Dear «Title» «Last_Name»,

My name is Fr. Matthew Mankowski and I am a student priest pursuing a Doctorate Degree at St. Mary Seminary in Wickliffe, OH. As part of my doctoral studies, I need to conduct a survey among a select group of parishioners from different parishes in the Diocese of Youngstown, Ohio. This group of parishioners have been involved in the process of merging, closing or collaborating of parishes. On **June 22, 2015,** I mailed a survey to you along with a "Participation Intent Card".

For this study to be successful, I need a certain number of participants from each parish. If you wish to participate in my survey but were unable to provide your input so far, please complete the enclosed survey and return it to me in the self-addressed stamped envelope. You may also complete this survey online at https://www.surveymonkey.com/s/Mankowski.

If you do not wish to participate in this survey, please indicate your choice on the enclosed self-addressed stamped "Participation Intent Card" and return to me as soon as possible. Simply mark the box on the enclosed Participation Intent Card that says; "No, I will NOT participate in this survey."

I fully understand that we live very busy lives and that this survey requires time and effort on your part. Please, know that I am very grateful for your time and willingness to be a part of this study. I hope that with your input, I will be able to analyze the data and develop a pastoral plan of assistance for parishioners and pastors who are involved in the process of merging, closing or collaborating of parishes.

Sincerely Yours in Christ,

Fr. Matthew Mankowski

Appendix N.
Thank You Letter

Rev. Matthew Maciej Mankowski, M.A., M. Div., D. Min. Cand.
Work Phone: (330) 821-5760
Cell Phone: (330) XXX-XXXX
E-mail: xxxxxxxx@aol.com
427 East Broadway Street, Alliance, OH 44601

August 6, 2015

«Title» «1st_Name» «Last_Name»
«Street_Address»
«City», «State» «Zip_Code»

Dear «Title» «Last_Name»,

I want to take this opportunity to sincerely thank you for completing the Informational Survey for my Doctor of Ministry Research. The response and feedback I have received has been overwhelming. I appreciate your honesty and candidness. The information gathered will be analyzed by me in order to determine how the merging, closing and collaborating of parishes in the Diocese of Youngstown, Ohio has affected, parishes, parishioners, pastors and the community at large. My hope is to develop a pastoral plan based on the best and worst practices in order to provide assistance for parishioners, pastors and parish leaders who may be a part of such a process in the future.

Please know that your identity will be kept completely confidential. In my study and analysis of the survey, I will use fictitious names for all participants. In the event that I publish this work or refer to it in a written and published form, I will continue to use pseudonyms and I may alter some identifying details to further protect your anonymity.
I am very grateful for your time and willingness to be a part of this study. May God continue to bless you and watch over you in the days that are yet to come.

Sincerely Yours in Christ,

Fr. Matthew Mankowski

Appendix O.
Link to Complete Survey Results

The document outlining all of the Research Book Survey results can be viewed at:
http://www.stjoseph-alliance.org/transition

Click on Appendix O

ANNOTATED BIBLIOGRAPHY

Arbuckle, Gerald A. *Catholic Identity or Identities? Refounding Ministries in Chaotic Times.* Collegeville, MN: Liturgical Press, 2013.

The Catholic Church of today faces many challenges connected with the postmodern culture, individualism, secularism, and secularization. Preserving Catholic identity in the fields of education and health care (Catholic universities and hospitals), as well as by the Catholic organizations providing social services, has been a serious challenge of our present postmodern age. Catholic leaders and the Catholic faithful need to search for new alternatives – new expressions of the Catholic identity on the personal and the institutional levels. Identities change along with the context in which they exist: history, power, and culture. The mission of Jesus must also be the mission of the Church while trying to find new ways for evangelization and the engagement with the postmodern world.

Arbuckle, Gerald A. *Culture, Inculturation, and Theologians: A Postmodern Critique.* Collegeville, MN: Liturgical Press, 2010.

Myths and symbols associated with different cultures, customs and traditions have significant influence on the formation of personal, group and cultural identities. An in-depth understanding of a particular culture and its functioning traditions is essential in the process of studying and analyzing cultural differences and the existing systems of values and core beliefs. Liturgical worship experiences can serve as an excellent starting point in the course of a deeper understanding of the lives of people rooted in local culture and traditions.

Arbuckle, Gerald A. *Refounding the Church: Dissent for Leadership.* Maryknoll, NY: Orbis Books, 1996.

Gerald Arbuckle dedicated his life to social anthropology. Arbuckle has been committed to helping church leaders evaluate various models of being a church in the post-modern culture. These characteristics formed his vision for the future of the Catholic Church. This text presents possible alternatives to the existing model of the Church. Fostering "responsible dissent," by searching for new alternatives of being a church community based on the mission of Jesus and the Gospel values are explored here. Catholic faithful living in the postmodern culture need be aware of the problems connected with the restorationism movement. The campaign to bring the pre-Vatican II model of Church back to life presents many issues. Modern day witch hunts, secrecy, authoritarian silence of the "unorthodox theologians" and manipulation of some members of the hierarchy are just a few of these problems. The Church is in dire need of the new evangelization based on a creative imagination, dialog, honesty, transparency, and accountability. The Catholic Church needs to create a clear vision for the future and empower the lay faithful in the process of applying the transformative model of leadership.

Archdiocese of Milwaukee, Office for Planning and Councils, *"Parish Merger Process."* http://www.archmil.org/ArchMil/Resources/ParPln/ParishMergerProcess-ALL2012 071.pdf (accessed October 20, 2014).

Pastors and parish leaders involved in mergers and clusters will find this plan to be an indispensable tool used in the process of planning and implementation of different consolidation stages. The document is an excellent step by step guide covering a broad range of subjects in regards to the pastoral, administrative, canonical, practical, legal, environmental and human resources areas of parish life and ministry. Anyone involved in the process of merging will greatly benefit from this practical and easy to use resource.

Archdiocese of Philadelphia, *"Guided by Faith Workbook: Cluster Pastoral Planning Process, September 1997."* http://archphila.org/pastplan/PDF/clusterworkbook.pdf (accessed October 20, 2014).

Aimed at the spiritual renewal of the Catholic faithful despite the declining number of diocesan and religious priests, the Archdiocese of Philadelphia issued the first of many pastoral plans for all existing parishes. This diocesan plan is a very helpful and practical tool for pastors and parish leaders who wish to examine the vitality of their parishes while being involved in the merger process. Parish leaders who do not have much experience in the areas of merging or closing of parishes will greatly benefit from this step by step guidance plan.

Archdiocese of Philadelphia, *"Characteristics Found in Vital Parishes, Spring 2003."* http://archphila.org/pastplan/PDF/VitalParish.pdf (accessed October 20, 2014).

People in leadership positions who work for culturally and economically diverse Catholic parishes will find this plan to be an indispensable parish evaluation tool that covers essential areas of parish life and ministry. Catholic parishes are encouraged to live in accordance with their missions, as well as a clear vision for the future. Parish pastoral councils will greatly benefit from this practical and easy to use tool, especially in the process of developing specific goals for the future of the church community. While developing a pastoral plan for the future, the seven fundamental areas of parish life must be taken into consideration. The fundamental areas are worship, Christian community, evangelization, teaching, service, leadership, and stewardship.

Archdiocese of Philadelphia, *"Call to Conversion and Holiness, In-Depth Evaluation of Parish Life, Fall 2011."* http://archphila.org/pastplan/PDF/InDepthEval.pdf (accessed October 20, 2014).

Presented here is one of the best available evaluation tools regarding various aspects of parish life. Parish church communities of today have been significantly affected by the drastic changes in the demographics of the Catholic population and the continuous decline in the numbers of available priests. With the dwindling financial resources and the number of parishioners involved in the life of their church communities, some parishes need to take an honest look at their missions and vitality. This plan serves as an excellent resource providing a step by step guide for pastors and parish leaders faced with matters concerning parish planning and parish evaluation.

Bauer, John. *"Communicate, Admit Mistakes and 30 Other Merging Lessons Learned." The Catholic Spirit,* September 8, 2010. http://thecatholicspirit.com/archdiocese /archdiocese-planning-process/communicate-admit-mistakes-and-30-other-merging-lessons-learned/. (accessed June 30, 2014).

Fr. Bauer shares valuable lessons learned by him and various priests personally involved in the process of merging, closing and collaborating of parishes in the Diocese of St. Paul and Minneapolis, Minnesota. Particular emphases are given here to the ongoing communication between parish leaders, parishioners, and diocesan representatives. The more communication takes place between all parties involved in the process of merging, closing and collaborating, the better. It is also important to inquire from parishioners about their preferred way of receiving information and communication from the pastor and the parish leadership team. When faced with the challenges associated with merging and closing parishes, precious elements should be observed. Parish and diocesan leadership must be present and accessible to the people. A timeline with benchmarks must be developed. Parish committees are to be formed to oversee the details connected with the process.

Bausch, William J. *The Parish of the Next Millennium.* Mystic, CT: Twenty-Third Publications, 1997.

How will the parish of the new millennium look? Analyzing the social and cultural trends and changes affecting the Catholic Church in the United States, Bill Baush attempts to book a vision for the future with particular emphasis on the challenges influencing the lives of the Catholic faithful. Cardinal Newman's concept of the three functions of the church were kingly, priestly and prophetic. Bill Baush emphasizes that all three concepts must exist in order to form a healthy church that serves the needs of all of her members, lay and ordained.

Berger, Teresa, ed. *Liturgy in Migration: From the Upper Room to Cyberspace.* Collegeville, MN: Liturgical Press, 2012.

This book edited by Teresa Berger is a compilation of different essays and articles reflecting the subject of liturgical migration of worship customs, hymns and traditions that function in many different places around the world. Various authors who contributed their articles and essays fort his book discuss a multitude of subjects connected with the liturgical celebrations and their formation throughout ancient and modern history of the Roman Catholic and Eastern Churches. This book is an excellent source of information describing the journey of God and God's people through liturgical worship experiences and popular customs and traditions.

Bramwell, Bevil. "The Theology of Church Closing." *Priest* 56 (May 2000): 41-43.

In this article, Bevil Bramwell presents and discusses several key reasons associated with church closing. Among essential reasons he mentions "shifts in demographics, impossible economic situations and the decline in the number of priests available to serve." (p. 41) The author provides some valuable answers and observations regarding the following questions: What does it mean to be a member of a church community? Also, How strong is the role of the faith in the lives of church community members? The Church is presented here as the undeniable mediator of God's salvation for God's people. "The Church mediates the grace and the truth of Christ." (p. 42) The role of a church community, especially, a local church community, is to hand down God's revelation to God's people for the salvation of all believers. When local churches close, we must always remember that we are a part of a larger body called the diocesan and Universal Church.

Cafardi, Nicholas P. "Closing Churches, Merging Institutes and Dividing Dioceses: Developments in Church Property Since 1983." *Canon Law Society of America* 52 (1990): 222-234.

The author of this article looks carefully at church property laws in comparison with the civil property laws. This article presents in detail different cannons that refer to the effects of closing and merging of Catholic churches. Insights are given regarding church property laws that are clear and easy to understand. Issues addressed are; who has the authority to close a parish, what is the process for such action to take place, and what criteria are most important for closure or merger to take place. One of the most revealing points of this article is a reminder that: "parish property is not diocesan property. The bishop cannot just take parish assets and use them for diocesan purposes or the debts of another parish." (p. 225)

Code of Canon Law: Latin-English Edition. Washington, DC: Canon Law Society of America, 1995.

The Code of Canon Law contains the official norms and regulations regarding the structure of the Catholic Church. The role of the Church hierarchy, juridic acts, duties and rights of the people of God both lay and ordained are also contained in this document. The Code of Canon Law also contains the norms and regulations of the sacraments of the church, the temporal goods of the Church, sanctions, trials, and procedures. Of particular interest for the main subject of this book are canons 121-123 regarding the public juridic person and the allocation of the parish property and temporary goods in cases of merged or closed parishes. In addition, Canon 515, §2 underlines the authority of the diocesan bishop "to erect, suppress or alter parishes."

Conference for Pastoral Planning and Council Development, 2003 National Study of Parish Reorganization. *"Some Key Findings About Parish Reconfigurations."* Future Church, http://futurechurch.org/save-our-parish-community/save-our-parish-community/resource/ save-our-parish-community (accessed March 18, 2014).

For twenty-six years, Future Church has been promoting a call for more collaboration, openness and active involvement of the lay faithful in the life and ministry of the Roman Catholic Church. Future Church endorses changes in the hierarchal structures of the Church, her governance and her leadership positions limited to the male clergy only. The key findings about parish reconfiguration are based on the 2003 National Study of Parish Reorganization published by the Conference for Pastoral Planning and Council Development. The results of this study show a significant increase in number of closed, merged and clustered parishes in the Northeast and Midwest parts of the U.S. between 1995 and 2005. The same study demonstrates changes in models of pastoral leadership. During the same period of time forty-two percent of U.S. dioceses replaced a resident pastor with a parish director (in accordance with Canon 517, §2). In addition, thirty-eight percent of U.S. dioceses replaced a resident pastor with a non-resident pastor. Shortage of priests and demographic changes in the U.S. Catholic populations are quoted as key factors affecting parish reconfiguration.

Coriden, James A. *The Parish in Catholic Tradition: History, Theology, and Canon Law*. Mahwah, N.J.: Paulist Press, 1997.

This book is an excellent resource of valuable information for anyone interested in the biblical origins, historical canonical, and theological aspects of local church communities called parishes in the Catholic tradition. The influence of the Roman culture, clearly visible in the organizational structure and customs of the early church communities gives great insight into the life of Christians and their faith practice in the Roman Empire. The theology of a local church community, parish membership, rights and obligations as well as the relationship between a local parish and a particular church called a diocese have been presented and discussed in great detail.

Diocese of Madison & The Reid Group, The Office for Planning, *"Trusting in the Spirit."* http://www.madisondiocese.org/LinkClick.aspx?fileticket=gIZZqyzqjQ%3 D&tabid=737&mid=2095 (accessed on June 30, 2014).

This online reference is by far one of the most practical and detailed plans regarding the merging, clustering and closing of parishes. As a result of the Diocese of Madison's diocesan-wide process of strategic planning, strategies were implemented to aid parish leaders and parishioners which benefit all people involved. This excellent resource covers a multitude of subjects and issues connected with the mergers and closures of Catholic parishes. Of particular interest are topics connected with the areas of accounting, finances and administration as well as the sacramental and canonical aspects reflecting the lives of parishes going through transitions.

Denk, J. Michael. "Sojourn, a Temporary Stay: for Those Struggling With Merging or Closing Parishes." *Priest* 68, no. 8 (August 2012): 13-16.

As members of a parish community, we form "a community of sojourners – a people who stay temporarily at places along the journey to Eternal Life." (p. 15) Parishes and Churches are not our final destinations, but rather temporary places of worship where our faith in nurtured through the reception of the sacraments. Just as Abraham put his faith and trust in God who led him into the unknown, so must people in transition allow God to lead them into a new church community where the Kingdom of God is being realized. Faith in God's loving care and guidance is necessary for any transition in the life of a church community to be successful and life-giving.

Duffy, Eugene. "Clustering Parishes II: The Theology." *Furrow* 61 (June 2010): 343-356.

The practical details concerning parish clusters require solid theological foundation built on an ecclesiology of communion, a renewed Trinitarian image of God, an inclusive theology of the priesthood based on collegiality, a spirituality of collaboration and a renewed vision for the parish life and ministry. The "old," image of an authoritarian God, a heartless judge withdrawn from the people, no longer applies. Our image of God has a direct influence on our approach and relationships with other people. The Trinitarian Image of God supports the notions of mutuality, dynamic love, reciprocity, and collaboration. Such an image is a perfect reflection and an example to follow for parishes engaged in the process of a merger or a cluster relationship. Clusters need to be perceived as a communion of communions under the guidance of a local minister/pastor ((lay or ordained), who is in communion with the diocesan bishop. The diocesan bishop, in turn, is in communion with the pope and the other members of episcopal college. Through the sharing of resources and the promotion of collaboration, parishes become a visible sign of Christ's presence in the world.

Easter, Opal. "Pastoral Advice on Parish Closures and Mergers in the African American Community." *New Theology Review* vol. 22, Issue 3 (August 2009): 25-35.

Opal Easter provides very pastoral and valuable advice for parish closures and mergers based on the experience of African American Church communities in the Archdiocese of Chicago. The phenomena of merging and closing of Catholic churches poses the need to assess the viability of all Catholic parishes in the US as they continue to engage actively in Jesus' mission. The challenges of closures and mergers affect pastors, bishops, parish staff, and parishioners. Four issues of great importance must be taken into consideration while implementing various parish reconfiguration plans: "transparency, pastoral care of the adults, pastoral care of the youth and parishioner participation." (p. 26) In any reconfiguration plan, attentiveness to people's pastoral, emotional and spiritual needs and their active involvement in the process of merger or closure are unignorable essential elements.

Francis, Mark R. *Local Worship. Popular Religion and the Liturgy*. Collegeville, MN: Liturgical Press, 2014.

This book is a wonderful source of valuable information for those interested in the early Christians. The customs, worship celebrations, as well as tradition and beliefs connected with the popular piety of the Church, are presented within this text. Mark Francis has a unique ability to make the ancient Roman Culture and its influence on the early Christianity come alive in this text. In this book, he illustrates an excellent example of enculturation and acculturation that continue to live on through a local worship experience in a globalized Church. This book is an excellent study source, especially in regards to the formation and development of the so-called Roman Rite in the Catholic Church.

Gallagher, Maureen. *Continuing the Journey: A Book for Parishes in Transition*. Kansas City, MO: Sheed & Ward, 1988.

Dealing with a loss of a parish due to a closure merger or clustering efforts can evoke many feelings and traumatic emotions. Many experts on the subject compare the loss of a parish community to a loss which is usually associated with the death of a loved one. Maureen Gallagher's book aims at providing practical advice and step by step guidance through the different stages of grief and loss. Remembering stories from the past, naming feelings and emotions, finding hope, dealing with problems and changes, and creating a vision for the future are just some of the suggestions presented in this resource. Lay and ordained parish leaders who find themselves serving in Catholic parishes going through serious changes can significantly benefit from the guidance and practical parish rituals of transition contained in this book.

Ganim, Carole, ed. *Shaping Catholic Parishes: Pastoral Leaders in the 21ˢᵗ Century*. Chicago: Loyola Press, 2008.

Lay and ordained parish leaders, who are engaged in various areas of parish ministry, face many challenges. As Catholic parishes become more diverse, the needs of the faithful become increasingly complex. Emerging models of pastoral leadership and parish ministry emphasize essential characteristics sought by people who wish to be a part of a modern church community. The characteristics sought are as follows: to be welcoming, to be open to collaboration, to be ethical, to be respectful of the dignity of each person, to be pastoral and nurturing, and to be prophetic. Parish church communities wishing to reach out to potential followers of Christ, need to be mission and vision driven. They also need to be ecumenical, evangelistic and promoting social justice as well as outreach to a larger community.

Goshay, Charita. "Diocese Releases Plan; Some Area Churches to Merge." *Canton Repository,* May 28, 2010.

On May 28, 2010, the Catholic Diocese of Youngstown released its reconfiguration plan regarding the merging and closing of its 112 Catholic parishes. Quoting demographic changes which affect the Catholic population in Northeast Ohio and the declining number of priests who experience work overload in parish ministry, Bishop George V. Murry deemed it necessary to introduce the parish reconfiguration plan. The envisioned plan reduced the number of existing parishes from 112 to 87. The majority of the twenty-five parishes most affected by the plan have been merged or entered into collaboration with another parish. A few parishes experienced the actual closure and the sale of parish property.

Gray, Mark M., Cidade, Melissa and Gautier, Mary L. *The Changing Face of U.S. Catholic Parishes: Emerging Models of Pastoral Leadership Series.* Washington, DC: National Association for Lay Ministry, 2011.

In 2009 the five Catholic national ministerial organizations employed the services of the Center for Applied Research in the Apostolate. The aim of the research was to gather and analyze data concerning parish life and ministry, emerging models of parish leadership and the future trends in the U.S. Catholic Church affecting the lay and ordained faithful and their Catholic identity. The face of the U.S. Catholic Church has changed dramatically in the last decade. The number of Catholic parishes in Northeast and Midwest significantly declined between 2000 and 2010 by 1,359 parishes – a decline of 7.1 percent. During the same period of time the number of diocesan priests declined by eleven percent. The demographic changes in the U.S. Catholic population and the shortage of priests affect parish changes. While small parishes cease to exist, the formation of the mega churches has become a reality. The more active participation and engagement of the lay people in the life and ministries of the church has been on the rise in the last decade. Their involvement in parish leadership roles and church governance creates new models of pastoral leadership for the future.

Harris, Joseph Claude. "The Disturbing Trends Behind Parish Closings." *America* Vol. 192, Issue 15 (May 2, 2005): 11-14.

Based on the demographics and the financial stability /vitality of Catholic parishes in Boston, the Archdiocese decided to close twenty-five percent of existing parishes. The shortage of priests, poor conditions of parish buildings and property and the lack of financial stability are cited as contributing factors for the closures and mergers of parishes. Similar reasons have been mentioned in Catholic dioceses around the United States: Fargo, N.D., Toledo, OH., and Detroit, MI. Shifts in the demographics of the U.S. Catholic population and the growing number of Latino-Catholics are two other significant trends that cannot go unnoticed. Parishes have been closing in the mid-west portion of the United States. However, they have been rapidly growing in the sun belt portion of the U.S. Lay members of the church, permanent deacons and professed religious men and women have been asked to serve as parish administrators. Moreover, many priests have been entrusted with a challenging ministry in multiple parishes.

Hater, Robert, J. *The Catholic Parish: Hope for the Changing World.* New York: Paulist Press, 2004.

There are many different challenges facing Catholic parishes in our post-modern world. The organizational structure, management styles and a vast array of parish ministries are in the process of an ongoing change in order to best serve the needs of diverse parishioners and members of a broader community where parishes are located. Empowering lay people for church ministry, creating a welcoming parish culture as well as developing a clear vision for the future are just a few important ideas presented in this excellent resource. An ongoing need for the New Evangelization and Jesus' call to serve one another in the spirit of Christian love and compassion must be at the very center of parish life and ministries.

Hilliard, Linda M., and Gretchen J. Switzer. *Finishing with Grace: A Guide to Selling, Merging, or Closing Your Church.* United States: Booklocker.com, 2010.

Both authors share their vast exposure and experience regarding the subjects of selling, merging and closing of Christian churches. Together they created an easy to follow and a very informative manual for pastors and lay church leaders. People who have been entrusted with the task of overseeing the structural changes affecting their respective church congregations will find this book as a very helpful resource guiding them through the different stages of the process of merging and closing of church congregations. This practical guide provides many important ideas and recommendations for church leaders and congregations in transition.

Hodge, Dean R. and Jewell, Marti R. *The Next Generation of Pastoral Leaders: What the Church Needs to Know.* Chicago, IL: Loyola Press, 2010.

While developing a vision for the future of different parish communities through the planning process, it is of great importance to take into account the mission of the local and the universal church. The needs and various gifts of young adults who search for new ways of being involved in the life and ministry of parish churches need to be acknowledged, explored and nurtured by pastors and parish leaders. Forming intentional disciples out of young Catholics in the twenty-first century is a crucial step in the process of sharing of our Catholic faith and empowering those who wish to get actively involved in pastoral ministry. The present generations of young Catholics, Gen X, Y and the Netgeners, are characterized as being better educated than previous generations, more affluent and more diverse socially, economically and ethnically or culturally. Such reality requires a vast array of evangelization efforts and new models of being a church community in the world.

Holmes, Paul A. *A Pastor's Toolbox: Management Skills for Parish Leadership.* Collegeville, MN: Liturgical Press, 2014.

Many pastors and parish leaders will find this book to be of great help to them in various areas of parish life and ministry. This book reminds seasoned Pastors as well as those newly appointed about the three fundamental aspects of their priestly service. The three fundamentals of priestly service are: *the munera Christi,* to be a priest (to sanctify), to be a prophet (to preach and to teach) and to be a king (to govern with love, mercy, and compassion). Much advice is given within this text by both lay and ordained people. Areas of parish life, such as budgets and finances, coaching of employees and staff members, risk management, fundraisers, transparency, the power of delegation, parish pastoral planning and the creating of a vision for the future are all topics within this book.

Howes, Robert G. *Bridges: Towards the Inter-Parish Regional Community...Deaneries, Clusters, Plural Parishes.* Collegeville, MN: Liturgical Press, 1998.

Based on the example of the diocese of Joliet, IL, Robert Howes shares his insights regarding the evaluation of a parish viability in light of the declining number of priests and the shifts in the demographics of the U.S. Catholic population. Open dialogue, parish planning, and management, as well as an ongoing collaboration based on the sharing of personnel and various resources among neighboring parishes, are indispensable elements for parish communities designated to be a part of a cluster or a merger.

Jervis, Rick. *"Faithful Fight for Church." USA Today,* May 07, 2008.

The Catholic Archdiocese of New Orleans like many other dioceses and archdioceses in the United States announced the closures and mergers of its thirty-three parishes. This decision reduced the number of existing parishes from 142 to 109. As many as twenty-five parish churches had been destroyed by Hurricane Katrina in 2005. In the aftermath of such a devastating natural disaster, thousands of Catholics moved out of the city area while others were relocated to different states and cities by the government. The declining numbers of parishioners and

Catholic priests in the area have been cited as main reasons for mergers and closures of parishes in New Orleans. The closing of Catholic parishes affects entire neighborhoods and limits the social outreach to those who need help and assistance.

Jewell, Marti. R. *"Linking Parishes: 6 Strategies for the Future: Creative Ways to Meet Today's Challenges."* Emerging Models. http://emergingmodels.org/wp-content/uploads/2012/05/ Linking- Parishes-Article.pdf (accessed March 18, 2014).

There are two main factors contributing to the need for linking and merging of parishes. The first reason is the declining number of priests actively involved in parish ministry. The second reason is the change in the demographics of the US Catholics. The number of Catholics living in the northeast is decreasing due to the movement of the Catholic population to the southern and the western parts of the country. In addition, there are increasing numbers of parishes which share a priest and also the growing numbers of parishes with a non-resident pastor.

Jewell, Marti R. and Ramey, David A. *The Changing Face of Church: Emerging Models of Parish Leadership.* Chicago: Loyola Press, 2010.

Modern-day Catholic parishes face numerous pressures and challenges. In addition parish leaders are faced with different ongoing problems including; financial deficit issues, the changing demographics of the Catholic population and parish restructuration process through mergers, clusters, and closures. Such serious challenges have a tremendous impact on the vitality of Catholic parishes in the United States. "Doing business as usual mentality," cannot and must not be applied any longer in the face of the declining numbers of priests and religious men and women. Lay and ordained Catholics need to take a fresh look at their call to discipleship and get actively involved in "the intentional parish planning and visioning." New forms of lay pastoral leadership are emerging in the life of many Catholic parish communities: sacramental ministers, parish life coordinators, lay parish administrators, lay parish assistants, lay pastoral associates and lay pastoral leaders.

Long-Garcia, J.D. "The Need For Closure." *U.S. Catholic* Vol. 75 Issue 10 (October 2010): 12-17.

Changing locks on church doors by the diocesan officials before the due date for the closing of a Catholic parish will create more anger and fury among church members then any good. Parishioners will fight and oppose such decisions, especially if made without due process and effective communication. The Archdiocese of Boston is a perfect example of such reality. Parish reconfiguration process must be built on transparency, collaboration, and pastoral sensitivity. The need for a due process is undeniable and pastorally wise. Closing vibrant parishes in order to pay off the victims of clergy sexual abuse is unacceptable in the eyes of both lay and ordained members of the church. Parish closures and merger will continue to be a part of a Catholic parish life and service into the future. However, the way through which this undeniable reality is being communicated and executed can either cause much harm or renew the faith of church members who find themselves to be in transition.

Long-Garcia, J. D. and Kira Dault. *"What's the Difference Between Closing a Parish and Closing a Church?" U.S. Catholic,* October 22, 2013. Accessed on March 18, 2014 and June 30, 2014.
http://www.madisondiocese.org/LinkClick.aspx?fileticket=gIZZ qyz-qjQ%3D&tabid=737&mid=2095).

Is there a difference between closing a church and closing a parish? The conviction of this article's authors is that there is a fundamental difference between these two entities. The former refers mostly to a physical building consecrated and designated for religious purposes. The later refers to a community of believers who may find themselves worshiping in more than one church building and under the pastoral guidance of one pastor. Canons 515 (bishop's authority to "erect, suppress or alter parishes") and 1222 (reasons for the closure of a church building) are discussed and presented here in detail.

Mogilka, Mark and Wiskus, Kate. *Pastoring Multiple Parishes: Emerging Models of Pastoral Leadership Book Series.* Chicago: Loyola Press, 2009.

Within the last few decades, multiple parish pastoring has become a norm for lay and ordained parish leaders in the United States. Recent surveys and reports on parish life indicate the development and emergence of new forms of pastoral care and leadership. Collaboration on all levels of church life and parish ministry, as well as a promotion of a mission-focused model of pastoral leadership, are indispensable elements capable of providing much-needed help and practical strategies for multiple parish ministries and parish leaders.

O'Malley, Michael. *"Youngstown Diocese Closes Buildings, But Merges Congregations."* The Cleveland Plain Dealer Blog, entry posted March 29, 2010, http://blog.cleveland.com /metro/ 2010/03/youngstown_diocese_closes_buil.html (accessed March 18, 2014).

Unlike the neighboring Catholic Diocese of Cleveland, the Youngstown Diocese decided to focus more attention on parish mergers and creating collaborative parish units instead of pushing for parish closures. The DOY Parish Planning Committee spent eighteen months formulating the first draft of the pastoral plan for Catholic parishes which fall under its canonical jurisdiction. The pastoral plan was based on parish self-evaluation and an active involvement of the lay faithful in the process of developing and altering the final working document.

Piderit, John J. and Morey, Melanie M. *Renewing Parish Culture: Building for a Catholic Future.* Collegeville, MN: Rowman & Littlefield Publishers, 2008.

Parish life, organizational structure, mission, vision, and role in the lives of culturally diverse parish members have been changing quite dramatically in the last 50 years. The ongoing decrease in the number of available priests, the shifts in the demographics of the U.S. Catholic population and the continuing decline in the number of men and women religious present a very serious challenge for the future. Most western countries, where Catholicism used to be strong, have been experiencing the same reality. The future of the Catholic Church, in the land of the free and home of the brave presents both challenges and reasons for hope and optimism. There is no doubt among researchers that Catholic culture, identity, and institutions have been influenced and challenged by the postmodern culture, and the values promoted by the secular society. Multiculturalism, the attitudes of young Catholic adults toward the Church and religion, in general, seem to indicate that there is a need for a deeper call to New Evangelization and a need to create a welcoming church community where diversity is being accepted and celebrated. The growing numbers of Catholic faithful and the emergence of new forms of parish lay leadership are just a few aspects of parish life and ministry in the 21st Century Catholic Church in the United States.

Provost, James H. "Some Canonical Considerations On Closing Parishes." *Jurist* 53 (February 1993): 362-370.

The subject of merging and closing of Catholic parishes has been discussed and carefully analyzed for the last three decades in the United States. Often mentioned reasons for this phenomenon are the shortage of available priests, the shifts in the demographics of the U.S. Catholic population, and the dwindling financial resources of Catholic parishes that face serious debt and financial emergencies. Canon Law of the Catholic Church ought to be applied when parishes are being merged or closed and when churches are being designated for secular usage. Although parishes are considered to be "public juridic persons," (c. 515, §3) with a perpetual nature (c. 120 §1), the diocesan bishop, after a consultation with the Presbyteral Council (c. 515 §2), has the authority to erect, suppress and alter any parish structure that falls under his canonical jurisdiction. When closing a parish or changing its structure the intentions of donors, founders and benefactors must be taken into consideration and respected in accordance with cannons 122-123. There is a significant difference between suppressing, altering or erecting of parishes and relegating an actual church building to profane use. (c. 1222, §2).

Ranier, Thom S. *Autopsy of a Deceased Church: 12 Ways to Keep Yours Alive.* Nashville, Tennessee: B&H Publishing Group, 2014.

There is much to be learned from the experiences of church communities that ceased to exist. This resource provides much-needed insights and lessons learned from churches that had to close their doors and disperse their congregations. Before many of these churches had died, there were many similar signs and patterns pointing to the upcoming doom. Unfortunately, while going through these traumatic changes and challenges, many church communities chose to live in denial, rather than dealing with the problems at hand. The death of a church usually takes place over an extended period of time, and the symptoms of their demise have a lot in common. Looking realistically at the signs of the times, naming the problems and creating a planned vision for the future along with an ongoing evaluation process for all church ministries and the overall mission of the church community are just a few essential steps desperately needed in the attempt to create a vital church.

Reidy, Maurice Timothy. "Closing Catholic Parishes: A Painful Process That Could Be Done Better." *Commonweal* 131 (September 10, 2004): 14-17.

The Archdiocese of Boston has been criticized by lay and ordained members, for closing twenty-five percent of its existing parishes. Many critics believe the reasons given for such a drastic move are not sufficient nor are they "the true reasons for closures." Some opponents of this decision maintain that certain parishes are being shut down in order to pay off the debt caused by legal litigation tied to the clergy sexual abuse of minors in Boston. The conviction of others is that "priests' shortage and poor management of parish finances and assets," are a cover up for the real reasons behind this decision. Lay people have the right to take an active role in the administration of Catholic parishes. A more consultative and a gradual process is strongly advised for the merging and closing of Catholic parishes. New forms of parish life and administration have been emerging and presently they are on the rise. Honest and ongoing communication with parish members is essential to this process.

Rivers, Robert S, CSP. *From Maintenance to Mission: Evangelization and the Revitalization of the Parish.* New York: Paulist Press, 2005.

Catholic parish communities involved in an active process of planning and envisioning of the future aimed at the New Evangelization and the Revitalization of the parish life and ministries will greatly benefit from this insightful and practical resource. Forming intentional disciples and helping Catholic parishes to move their direction from being maintenance oriented to become mission-driven communities are essential elements contributing to the effectiveness of the New Evangelization methods and the formation of intentional disciples for whom evangelization is a way of life.

Roberts, Tom. "Parish Closing Trauma." *National Catholic Reporter* Vol. 45 Issue 7 (January 23, 2009): 1-13.

There is hardly any doubt among people who experienced firsthand the painful reality of parish closing or merging that emotions run high when parishes are being suppressed, and congregations have been dispersed. From one U.S. Catholic diocese to another, various bishops have resorted to different methods of dealing with angry church members who refuse to accept their decision to close certain local parishes. In some dioceses, the Catholic faithful have been removed by police from the parish premises and manhandled by law enforcement representatives at the request of a local bishop. (Abp. Alfred Hughes in New Orleans) The shifts in the demographics of the U.S. Catholic population, the shortage of priests and severe financial problems in some parishes have been mentioned as the main reasons for closures and mergers of parishes. The restructuring of Catholic parishes in the U.S. as well as the emergence of new models of being a parish community especially in the areas of parish administration, life and ministry, will continue to grow and develop for a long time into the future.

Schiffer, Kathy. *"Benedict's Warning and Consolation: Changing Demographics Mean Closing Churches."* Kathy Schiffer' Blog, entry posted September 5, 2012. http://development.patheos.com/blogs/kathyschiffer/2012/09/benedicts-warning-and-consolation-changing-demographics-mean-closing-churches/ (accessed on February 1, 2015).

There is no doubt that the change in demographics has been a serious challenge for many Catholic parishes and dioceses in the United States. (The Archdioceses of Milwaukee and Detroit are being used here as examples.) Many parishes have been closed, merged or clustered. The declining number of available priests and the rising financial cost of running Catholic parishes and their different ministries are cited here as two major factors contributing to this serious problem. Some people believe that the mission of the Catholic Church may be fulfilled more efficiently through the combining of various parish resources and the restructuring of various parish ministries.

Schuth, Katarina. *Priestly Ministry in Multiple Parishes*. Collegeville, MN: Liturgical Press, 2006.

Nowadays more frequently than not ordained and lay leaders involved in pastoral ministry are being asked to serve in multiple parishes. This two-year study regarding the life and work of almost 1000 priests presents many valuable insights concerning the positive and the negative effects of ministry in multiple parish setting. Pastors and lay leaders offer their insight and share their personal experience in order to help future parish leaders become better equipped for the multiple parish ministries. Excellent practical advice is offered here especially for the newly assigned pastors and parish leaders. The information given here reflects the subjects of the spiritual and personal well-being of pastors, the concept of an active exercise of ministry and the subject of ministerial relationships and responsibilities.

Seitz, John C. *No Closure: Catholic Practice and Boston's Parish Shutdowns*. Cambridge, MA: Harvard University Press, 2011.

Based on the experience of merging and closing of Catholic parishes in the Archdiocese of Boston, which took place a decade ago, Tim Seitz presents profound insights into the Catholic identity of different parish members. Particular focus has been given here to the meaning of local parishes in the lives of the Catholic faithful. Subjects connected with the implementation of the Archdiocese of Boston reconfiguration plan called "Parish Closing Manual: Rebuilt My Church," range from grief management, suggested liturgical rituals for final sacramental celebrations, providing checklists and forms for parishes in transition as well as the struggle for power and control in Catholic church communities. Special attention is being given here to the negative feelings and emotions associated with the process of merging and closing of parishes.

Senn, Frank C. "When Churches Die." *Liturgy* 14 (1997): 51-55.

We are presented here with some valuable and practical insights concerning the process of a church closing. Frank C. Senn reminds his readers that most people experience being a part of a church community on a local level. "We experience the church locally, or we do not experience it at all." (p. 51) While dealing with "the death of a church," pastors and parish leaders must take into account people's feelings of loss, grief and anger. Before members of a dying church community come to terms and accept the fact that their church will no longer remain in existence, they must be given enough time to grieve and mourn. Dying church congregations just like dying people go through the following five stages: denial, anger, bargaining, depression and acceptance. Pastoral sensitivity is an essential element when implementing a "meaningful and therapeutic," ritual for closing of a church.

Sensing, Tim. *Qualitative Research: A Multi-methods Approach to Books for Doctor of Ministry Theses*. Eugene, OR: Wipf & Stock, 2011.

Tim Sensing provides indispensable guidance and advice for people pursuing the Doctor of Ministry Degree. Chapter by chapter, the reader becomes more acquainted with the requirements and the methodology expected from Doctor of Ministry students who are engaged in the process of writing their theological thesis. This practical guide reminds the Doctor of Ministry students about the need to connect their theological and theoretical chapters with the pastoral settings of their respective places of ministry. This step by step guide is presently one of the best resources for students enrolled in the Doctor of Ministry Program.

Serjak, Cynthia. "Leaving a Sacred Space: Closing a Church." *Pastoral Music* 33, no. 6 (2009): 31-33.

The author of this article recommends the use of Catholic Funeral Rites in the process of closing a church. The focal point in the ritual of closing a church should be a celebration of the life of the church community, her past customs, traditions, and history. When adopted with proper pastoral sensitivity, Catholic funeral rites shall help a grieving congregation to deal with loss and to look into the future with hope. Very often, shock, grief, and anger are associated with the church closing process and must be taking into account by pastors and parish leaders.   Listening to people's stories and celebrating together the last Eucharist as a church community are crucial elements of this process.

Sofield, Loughlan, S.T. and Juliano, Carroll, S.H.C.J. *Collaboration: Uniting Our Gifts in Ministry.* Notre Dame, IN: Ava Marie Press, 2000.

Discovering and affirming of all gifts given to the disciples and followers of Christ for the sake of continuing His mission in today's world and the process of building of God's Kingdom here and now require openness to dialogue and collaboration with lay and ordained parish leaders. Working together in partnership, empowering lay leaders and promoting a servant leadership model based on a collaborative ministry are indispensable methods through which modern-day leaders can become more adequately prepared to meet the present challenges facing Catholic parish communities in the United States.

Turabian, Kate L. *A Manual for Writers of Research Papers, Theses, and Dissertations: Chicago Style for Students and Researchers, Eighth Edition.* Chicago: University of Chicago Press, 2013.

This text is a resource for students and researchers using the Chicago Style in their academic writings. The book gives detailed examples of how to write their thesis in a methodological way. Instruction is also presented on how to cite different books, documents and publications in their footnotes, endnotes, and bibliography. Chapters 15-19 are of particular interest to the modern researcher who has access to online resources in audio and in video forms. These chapters provide help with unpublished sources and electronic sources along with websites, blogs, social networks and discussion groups.

The Vatican Collection: The Conciliar and Post Conciliar Documents, ed. Austin Flannery, vol. 1, Northport, NY: Costello, 1992.

Anyone who wishes to have a smooth and user-friendly access to all official documents approved by the Magisterium during the Second Vatican Council will greatly benefit from this book. In addition to the conciliar and post-conciliar documents included in this collection, there are many useful references to the original sources and writings that were used as a starting point for many of the encyclicals and official pronouncements of the Magisterium.

Weddell, Sherry A. *Forming Intentional Disciples: The Path to Knowing and following Jesus.* Huntington, IN: Our Sunday Visitor Publishing Division, 2012.

Sherry A. Weddell presents in her book a fascinating concept of transforming modern Catholics from being consumers and passive recipients of faith and sacraments into becoming intentional disciples of Jesus Christ. She proposes the use of five stages/thresholds for this process that include trust, curiosity, openness, spiritual seeking and, finally, becoming intentional disciples. When properly applied these thresholds are capable of helping Catholic faithful to move from their passive (dead) faith into the living faith based on a personal relationship with Jesus Christ. We are experiencing an era marked by an aggressive secularization, often expressed through the declining mass attendance and the continuous exodus of many Catholics from the institutional Church. This is primarily due to the lack of trust and confidence in the hierarchy, clergy sexual abuse scandals, lack of hospitality, acceptance and any kind of open dialog with the lay people. This book serves as a very timely and inspirational attempt aimed at transforming Catholic faithful from consumers into committed disciples of the Lord Jesus.

Weldon, Michael, O.F.M. *A Struggle for Holy Ground: Reconciliation and the Rites of Parish Closure.* Collegeville, MN: Liturgical Press, 2004.

Closed and merged parish communities should consider using this book as a valuable and easy to follow resource for parishes in transition. Of special interest are "Parish Closure Rites," which can provide significant help to parishioners who grieve the loss of their parish in similar ways as people who have lost a loved one due to death. There are three serious challenges currently affecting the Catholic faithful in the United States. These challenges are the changing demographics of the Catholic population in the United States, the declining number of priests and the lack of sufficient financial resources for the everyday operations of different parish communities

White, Michael, and Corcoran, Tom. *The Story of a Catholic Parish Rebuilt: Awakening the Faithful, Reaching the Lost, Making Church Matter.* Notre Dame, IN: Ave Maria Press, 2013.

Fr. Michael White and Tom Corcoran offer their valuable and practical advice, based on their pastoral experiences, to ordained and lay parish leaders who wish to breathe new life into their parish communities. Useful ideas expressed in this book to aid this complex process are the development of realistic vision and mission statements and concrete strategies for the renewal of parish life and the members of the parish. Challenging the "church people," (those who come to church and who are somewhat involved in the life of a parish) to become committed disciples of Jesus Christ is certainly an important and thought-provoking idea. Reaching out to "the lost and the unchurched people," are fundamental elements in the process of building a parish community of committed disciples who are open to restoration and revitalization of their parish.

White, Michael, and Corcoran, Tom. *Tools for Rebuilding: 75 Really, Really Practical Ways to Make Your Parish Better.* Notre Dame, IN: Ave Maria Press, 2013.

This book is a very practical and useful follow-up to the initial book called *"Rebuilt."* Both authors give their readers excellent advice based on their experience and the experience of those who are in a position of leadership in the

Catholic Church. Helpful ideas concerning the celebration of the sacraments and the Catholic worship experience are being given here as a way of improving the existing status quo. Lay and ordained parish leaders will actively benefit from this book, especially if they focus their attention on promoting hospitality and the formation of intentional disciples. Reaching out to the lost and to those who have left the Church needs to be an important part of this process. Both authors believe seeking the lost and challenging the church people are the essential pillars necessary for an effective process of evangelization.

Zech, Charles E. and Miller, Robert J. *Listening to the People of God: Closing, Rebuilding, and Revitalizing Parishes*. Mahwah, NJ: Paulist Press, 2008.

Both authors present here a very helpful and practical guide for Catholic parishes implementing organizational structure changes through the process of merger, suppression or creation of a new parish community. The lives of many parishes in the future will be significantly affected by the demographic changes, limited availability of Catholic priests and the changing expectations of the Catholic faithful. Corporate mergers, blended families, and successful parish mergers are important sources of practical information applied in the process of merging and closing of parishes.

CPSIA information can be obtained
at www.ICGtesting.com
Printed in the USA
BVOW09s1225231116

PP7634500001B/2/P

9 781539 751632